William Lowes Rushton

Shakespeare Illustrated by Old Authors

The first Part

William Lowes Rushton

Shakespeare Illustrated by Old Authors
The first Part

ISBN/EAN: 9783337063641

Printed in Europe, USA, Canada, Australia, Japan

Cover: Foto ©Thomas Meinert / pixelio.de

More available books at **www.hansebooks.com**

SHAKESPEARE ILLUSTRATED.

Floriferis ut apes in saltibus omnia libant,
Omnia nos itidem depascimur aurea dicta,
Aurea. perpetuâ semper dignissima vitâ.   13.

LUCRETIUS iii.

SHAKESPEARE

ILLUSTRATED BY OLD AUTHORS

BY

WILLIAM LOWES RUSHTON

OF GRAY'S INN, BARRISTER-AT-LAW

Corresponding Member of the Berlin Society for the Study of Modern
Languages: Author of 'Shakespeare a Lawyer,' 'Shakespeare's Legal
Maxims,' 'Shakespeare Illustrated by the Lex Scripta,' &c.

*Multa ignoramus quæ nobis non laterent si veterum lectio
nobis fuit familiaris.*—10 Co. 73.

THE FIRST PART.

LONDON:

LONGMANS, GREEN, AND CO.

1867.

LONDON
PRINTED BY SPOTTISWOODE AND CO.
NEW-STREET SQUARE

NOTICE.

— ✦ —

THIS SMALL VOLUME contains a few extracts from illustrations of SHAKESPEARE, contributed, since the year 1859, to the Berlin Society for the Study of Modern Languages, and published from time to time in the *Archiv für das Studium der neueren Sprachen und Literaturen.*

I will try to illustrate and explain many obscure passages and words and expressions of doubtful meaning in the Works of SHAKESPEARE by extracts from old authors: sometimes I will give my own explanations and offer suggestions for the consideration of the reader, but when the extracts themselves sufficiently illustrate and explain the passages selected, and the words and expressions therein contained, I will make no comment.

5 ESSEX COURT, TEMPLE:
Long Vacation, 1866.

SHAKESPEARE

ILLUSTRATED BY OLD AUTHORS.

———◆———

Bertram. Go with me to my chamber, and advise me.
I'll send her straight away : To-morrow
I'll to the wars, she to her single sorrow.
Parolles. Why, these balls bound; there's noise in it.
——'Tis hard ;
A young man, married, is a man that's marr'd ;
Therefore away, and leave her bravely ; go :
The king has done you wrong ; but, hush ! 'tis so.
            All's Well that Ends Well, Act ii. Sc. 3.

Shakespeare in this passage alludes to a
figure called Atanaclasis, or the Rebound, thus
described by Puttenham :

Ye have another figure which by his nature we may
call the Rebound, alluding to the tennis ball which.
being smitten with the racket, reboundes backe again,
and where the last figure before played with two words
somewhat like, this playeth with one word written all
alike, but carrying divers sences, as thus :

The maide that soone married is, soone marred is.

B

Or thus better, because married and marred be different
in one letter :

> To pray for you ever I cannot refuse,
> To pray upon you I should you much abuse.

Or as we once sported upon a countrey fellow who
came to runne for the best game, and was by his occupation a dyer, and had very bigge swelling legges :

> He is but course to run a course,
> Whose shankes are bigger then his thye,
> Yet is his lucke a little worse,
> That often dies before he dye.

Where ye see this word course and dye, used in divers
senses, one giving the Rebounde upon th' other.—*The
Arte of English Poesie*, 1589, Lib. iii.

And the reader will perceive that the line used
by Parolles,

> A young man married is a man that's marr'd,

resembles the line,

> The maid that soone married is soone marred is,

used by Puttenham, in his explanation of this
figure, the Rebound.

> *Par.* Younger than she are happy mothers made.
> *Cap.* And too soon marr'd are those so early made.
>> *Romeo and Juliet*, Act i. Sc. 2.

Capulet also probably alludes to the Rebound,
and to the line used by Puttenham.

> *Bion.* His daughter is to be brought by you to the
> supper.
> *Luc.* And then ?
> *Bion.* The old priest of Saint Luke's church is at
> your command at all hours.

Luc. And what of all this?

Bion. I cannot tell; expect they are busied about a counterfeit assurance: take you assurance of her, 'cum privilegio ad imprimendum solum:' to the church; take the priest, clerk, and some sufficient honest witnesses.

Taming the Shrew, Act iv. Sc. 4.

The words ' cum privilegio ad imprimendum solum,' which Shakespeare uses in this passage, are sometimes seen on the title-pages of old books announcing the sole privilege of printing them, thus:

The workes of Geffrey Chaucer newlye printed, wyth dyuers workes which were neuer in print before : As in the table more playnly doth appere. Cum Priuilegio ad imprimendum Solum. Prynted by John Reynes, dwellynge at the sygne of Saynte George, in Paul's Church-yarde, 1542.

And I think that Shakespeare uses them in a double, or rather in a covert sense. The infinitive of the Latin verb *imprimo*, *in* and *premo*, signifies to press. Biondello therefore says, in effect, ' take your assurance of her with the sole privilege of pressing her,' and this is an assurance taken in marriage ; so that the words, ' cum privilegio ad imprimendum solum,' are applicable to a man who issues a book from the press, and also to a man who takes a woman in marriage.

Ch. Just. I then did use the person of your father;
The image of his power lay then in me:
And, in the administration of his law,
Whiles I was busy for the commonwealth,
Your highness pleased to forget my place,
The majesty and power of law and justice,   .
The image of the king whom I presented,
And struck me in my very seat of judgement;
Whereon, as an offender to your father,
I gave bold way to my authority
And did commit you.

2 Henry IV., Act v. Sc. 2.

Injuria illata judici, seu locum tenenti regis, videtur
ipsi regi illata, maxime fiat in exercentem officium.—
COKE, 3 *Inst. I.*

Shakespeare in this passage probably refers
to this maxim, or to the law which it describes.
The Chief Justice says, ' When I did use the
person of your father, &c., you struck me in
my very judgment seat, whereon as an offender
to your father I did commit you;' and according to this maxim, an injury offered to a judge,
or one holding the place of the king, is considered to be offered to the king himself, especially if done during the exercise of the office
of a judge. Also Aristotle, speaking Περὶ
μειζόνων καὶ ἐλαττόνων ἀδικημάτων, says:

Ποῦ γὰρ οὐκ ἂν ἀδικήσειεν, εἴ γε καὶ ἐν τῷ δικαστηρίῳ;
—*Rhet.* Lib. i. 14.

Malcolm. If such a one be fit to govern, speak :
I am as I have spoken.
     Macduff.   Fit to govern !
No, not to live.—O nation miserable,
With an untitled tyrant bloody-scepter'd,
When shalt thou see thy wholesome days again ?
Since that the truest issue of thy throne
By his own interdiction *stands accursed,*
And does blaspheme his breed ?
             Macbeth, Act iv. Sc. 3.

In the second dialogue between the Doctor
and Student, Chapter LV., which contains 'the
eight questions of the Doctor, whether the
statute of 14th Edward the Third, of Sylva
cædua, stand with conscience,' are these words :

And it seemeth to stand hardly with conscience to re-
port so many to *stand accursed* for following of the said
stat. and of the said prescription as there do, and yet to
do no more than hath bin done to bring them out of it.

Of this old book, the Doctor and Student,
Coke says :

Dialogus inter sacræ Theologiæ Doctorem et Legis com-
munis Studiosum, anno 23 Henr. VIII. conscriptus fuit ab
authore appelato S. Germin, viro sine dubio prudente et
juris tum municipalis tum Civilis et Canonici satis perito.

Sam.   Gregory, o' my word, we'll not carry coals.
Gre.   No, for then we should be colliers.
Sam.   I mean, an we be in choler, we'll draw.
Gre.   Ay, while you live, draw your neck out of the
collar.
             Romeo and Juliet, Act i. Sc. 1.

Boy. Nym and Bardolph are sworn brothers in filching; and in Calais they stole a fire-shovel: I knew, by that piece of service, the men would carry coals.

Henry V., Act iii. Sc. 2.

In this trouble the earle of Ormond was greatlie aided by Sir William Wise Knight, a worshipfull gentleman, borne in the city of Waterford, who deserving indeed the praise of that great vertue, whereof he bare the name, grew to be of great credit in the court, and stood highlie in King Henric his grace, which he wholie used to the furtherance of his friends, and never abused to the annoiance of his foes. This gentleman was verie well spoken, mild of nature, with discretion stont, as one that in an upright quarell would *bear no coles*, seldome in an intricate matter gravelled, being found at all affaires to be of a pleasant wit.

Slender. All his successors gone before him hath done 't; and all his ancestors that come after him may: they may give the dozen white luces in their coat.

Shallow. It is an old coat.

Evans. The dozen white louses do become an old coat well; it agrees well, passant; it is a familiar beast to man, and signifies love.

Shallow. The luce is the fresh fish; the salt fish is an old coat.

Merry Wives of Windsor, Act i. Sc. 1.

Having lent the king his signet to seale a letter, who having powdred crimits ingrailed in the scale, Why, how now, Wise (quoth the king), what, hast thou lice here? And if it like your majestie, quoth Sir William, a louse is a rich cote, for by giving the louse, I part armes with the French King, in that he giveth the floure de lice. Whereat the King laughed to heare how

pretilie so biting a taunt (namlie proceeding from a
prince) was suddenlie turned to so pleasant a conceipt.—
A continuation of the Chronicles of Ireland, HOLINSHED.

Shakespeare seems to have been familiar with
Holinshed's Chronicles, and this passage may
have suggested the dialogue between Shallow,
Slender, and Evans.

Servant. My master preaches patience to him, while
His man with scissars *nicks him like a fool.*
　　　　　Comedy of Errors, Act v. Sc. 1.

Righte unsemely, on queynte manere,
He hym dight, as ye shall here.
A barber he callyd, withouten more,
And shove hym bothe behynd and before,
Quently endentyd, out and in ;
And also he shove half his chynne :
He seemyd a fole, that queynte sire,
Bothe by hede and by atyre.
　　　Weber's Metrical Romances, Vol. ii. p. 340.

Abergavenny. 　　　　　I do know
Kinsmen of mine, three at the least, that have
By this so sicken'd their estates, that never
They shall abound as formerly.
　　Buckingham. 　　　　　O, many
Have broke their backs with laying manors on them
For this great journey. What did this vanity,
But minister communication of
A most poor issue ?
　　　　King Henry VIII., Act i. Sc. 1.

So ridiculous, moreover, we are in our attires, and
for cost so excessive, that as Hierome said of old, Uno

filo villarum insunt pretia, uno lino decies sestertium
inseritur: 'Tis an ordinary thing to put a thousand
oaks and an hundred oxen into a suit of apparel, *to
wear a whole mannor on his back.*—BURTON's *Anatomy of
Melancholy*, Part iii. Sec. 2, Mem. 3. Subs. 3.

Hamlet. Sure, he, that made us with such large
  discourse,
Looking before, and after, gave us not
That capability and godlike reason
To fust in us unused.

Act iv. Sc. 4.

Gewiss, der uns mit solcher Denkkraft schuf
Voraus zu schaun und rückwärts, gab uns nicht
Die Fähigkeit und göttliche Vernunft,
Um ungebraucht in uns zu schimmeln.

SCHLEGEL.

The expression, 'looking before and after,'
which Shakespeare uses in Hamlet, is to be
found in the Iliad, and also in the Odyssey of
Homer:

ὁ γὰρ οἶος ὅρα πρόσσω καὶ ὀπίσσω.
Il. xviii. 250 ; *Od.* xxiv. 451.

der allein so vorwärts schaute wie rückwärts.
Il. Voss.

der allein vorwärts hinschauet und rückwärts.
Od. Voss.

οὐδέ τι οἶδε νοῆσαι ἅμα πρόσσω καὶ ὀπίσσω.
Il. i. 343.

Und nicht weiss er zu schauen im Geist vorwärts und
auch rückwärts.   *Il.* Voss.

And the reader will perceive that Schlegel, in translating that expression, uses almost the same words which Voss uses in translating those lines.

Macbeth.   Methought I heard a voice cry 'Sleep no more!
Macbeth does murder sleep,' the innocent sleep,
Sleep that knits up the ravell'd sleave of care,
The death of each day's life, sore labour's bath,
Balm of hurt minds, great nature's second course,
Chief nourisher in life's feast.

Act ii. Sc. 2.

ὦ φίλον ὕπνου θέλγητρον, ἐπίκουρον νόσου,
ὡς ἡδύ μοι προσῆλθες ἐν δέοντί γε.
ὦ πότνια λήθη τῶν κακῶν, ὡς εἶ σοφὴ
καὶ τοῖσι δυστυχοῦσιν εὐκταία θεός.   214.

EURIPIDES, Orestes.

Somne, quies rerum, placidissime Somne Deorum,
Pax animi, quem cura fugit, qui corda diurnis
Fessa ministeriis mulces, reparasque labori.

OVID, Met. xi. 623.

K. John.   The king is *moved*, and answers not to this.
Const.   O, be *removed* from him, and answer well.

King John, Act iii. Sc. 1.

Petrucio.   Myself am moved to woo thee for my wife.
Katharina.   Moved! in good time: let him that
moved you hither
Remove you hence: I knew you at the first
You were a moveable.

Taming the Shrew, Act ii. Sc. 1.

Nestor. With due observance of thy godlike seat,
Great Agamemnon, Nestor shall apply
Thy latest words. In the *reproof* of chance
Lies the true *proof* of men.

Troilus and Cressida, Act i. Sc. 3.

Anne. Fouler than heart can think thee, thou canst
make
No *excuse* current, but to hang thyself.
Glou. By such despair, I should *accuse* myself.
Anne. And, by despairing, shouldst thou stand
excused;
For doing worthy vengeance on thyself,
Which didst unworthy slaughter upon others.

Richard III., Act i. Sc. 2.

Launce. Thou shalt never get such a secret from me
but by a parable.
Speed. 'Tis well that I get it so. But, Launce, how
sayest thou, that my master is become a notable *lover*?
Launce. I never knew him otherwise.
Speed. Than how?
Launce. A notable *lubber*, as thou reportest him
to be.
Speed. Why, thou whoreson ass, thou mistakest me.

Two Gentlemen of Verona, Act ii. Sc. 5.

Ye have a figure by which ye play with a couple of
words or names resembling, and because the one seemes to
answere th' other by manner of illusion, and doth, as it
were, nick him, I call him the nicknamer. If any other
man can give him a fitter English name, I will not be
angrie, but I am sure mine is very neere the originall sence
of Prosonomasia, and is rather a by-name geven in sport,
than a surname geven of any earnest purpose. As Tiberius the Emperor, because he was a great drinker of wine
they called him by way of derision to his own name,

Caldius Biberius Mero, insteade of Claudius Tiberius
Nero; and so a jesting frier that wrote against Erasmus,
called him by resemblance to his own name, Erransmus,
and are maintained by this figure Prosonomasia, or the
nicknamer. But every name given in jest or by way of
a surname, if it do not resemble the true, is not by this
figure. Now, when such resemblance happens betweene
words of another nature, and not upon men's names, yet
doeth the Poet or maker finde prety sport to play with
them in his verse, specially the Comicall Poet and the
Epigrammatist. Sir Philip Sidney in a dittie plaide very
pretily with these two words, love and live, thus:

> And all my life I will confesse,
> The lesse I love, I live the lesse.

And ye in our Enterlude called the Woer, plaid with
these two words, *lubber* and *lover*, thus: the countrey
clowne came and woed a young maide of the Citie, and
being agreeved to come so oft, and not to have his
answere, said to the old nurse very impatiently:

> Iche pray you, good mother, tell our young dame,
> Whence I am come and what is my name;
> I cannot come a woing every day.

Quoth the nurse:

> They be *lubbers*, not *lovers*, that so used to say.

Or as one replyed to his mistresse charging him with
some disloyaltie towards her:

> Prove me, madame, ere ye fall to *reprove*;
> Meeke mindes should rather *excuse* than *accuse*.

Here the words prove and reprove, excuse and accuse,
do pleasantly encounter, and (as it were) mock one
another by their much resemblance; and this is by the

figure Prosonomasia, as well as if they were men's proper names, alluding to each other.—PUTTENHAM, *The Arte of English Poesie*, Lib. iii. Chap. 19.

The reader will perceive that Shakespeare plays with lover and lubber, excuse and accuse, and other words used by Puttenham in illustration of this figure.

———

Dromio E. She is so hot, because the meat is *cold*;
The meat is *cold*, because you come not *home*;
You come not *home*, because you have no *stomach*;
You have no *stomach*, having broke your fast.
But we that know what 'tis to fast and pray,
Are penitent for your default to day.
       Comedy of Errors, Act i. Sc. 2.

Rosalind. For your brother and my sister no sooner met, but they *looked*; no sooner *looked*, but they *loved*; no sooner *loved*, but they *sighed*; no sooner *sighed*, but they asked one another the *reason*; no sooner knew the *reason*, but they sought the remedy : and in these degrees have they made a pair of stairs to marriage, which they will climb incontinent, or else be incontinent before marriage : they are in the very wrath of love, and they will together; clubs cannot part them.—Act v. Sc. 2.

Ye have a figure which, as well by his Greeke and Latine originals, and also by allusion to the maner of a man's gate, or going, may be called the marching figure, for after the first steppe all the rest proceede by double the space; and so in our speech, one word proceeds double to the first that was spoken, and goeth, as it were, by strides or paces. It may as well be called the *clyming* figure, for clymax is as much to say as a ladder, as in one of our epitaphes, shewing how a very meane man, by his wisdome and good fortune, came to great estate and dignitie:

His vertue made him wise, his wisedome brought him
    wealth;
His wealth won many friends, his friends made much
    supply:
Of aides in weale and woe, in sicknesse and in health,
Thus came he from a low to sit in seat so hye.

Or, as Ihean de Mehune, the French poet:

> Peace makes plentie, plentie makes pride;
> Pride breeds quarrell, and quarrel brings warre;
> Warre brings spoile, and spoile povertie;
> Povertie pacience, and pacience peace:
> So peace brings warre, and warre brings peace.

PUTTENHAM, *The Arte of English Poesie*, Lib. iii. 19.

In these passages Shakespeare may refer to Clymax, or the marching figure. Rosalind makes 'one word proceed double to the first that was spoken,' thus—' Your brother and my sister no sooner met, but they looked; no sooner looked, but they loved: no sooner loved, but they sighed; no sooner sighed, but they asked one another the reason; no sooner knew the reason, but they sought the remedy;' and she says besides, 'in these degrees have they made a pair of *stairs* to marriage which they will *climb*;' and Puttenham says, 'It may be

called the clyming figure, for clymax is as
much as to say as a *ladder*,' &c.

     Tranio. Mi perdonate, gentle master mine,
I am in all affected as yourself;
Glad that you thus continue your resolve
To suck the sweets of sweet philosophy.
Only, good master, while we do admire
This virtue and this moral discipline,
Let 's be no stoicks, nor no stocks, I pray;
Or so devote to Aristotle's checks,
As Ovid be an outcast quite abjured:
Talk logic with acquaintance that you have,
And practise rhetoric in your common talk;
Music and poesy use to quicken you;
The mathematics, and the metaphysics,
Fall to them as you find your stomach serves you:
No profit grows, where is no pleasure ta'en;—
In brief, sir, study what you most affect.
        Taming the Shrew, Act i. Sc. 1.

Φανείη δ' ἂν τοῦτο καὶ ἐκ τοῦ συνῳκειῶσθαι τῶν ἡδονῶν
ἑκάστην τῇ ἐνεργείᾳ ἣν τελειοῖ. συναύξει γὰρ τὴν ἐνέργειαν
ἡ οἰκεία ἡδονή· μᾶλλον γὰρ ἕκαστα κρίνουσι καὶ ἐξακριβοῦσιν
οἱ μεθ' ἡδονῆς ἐνεργοῦντες, οἷον γεωμετρικοὶ γίνονται οἱ χαίροντες τῷ γεωμετρεῖν, καὶ κατανοοῦσιν ἕκαστα μᾶλλον, ὁμοίως
δὲ καὶ οἱ φιλόμουσοι καὶ φιλοικοδόμοι καὶ τῶν ἄλλων ἕκαστοι
ἐπιδιδόασιν εἰς τὸ οἰκεῖον ἔργον χαίροντες αὐτῷ. συναύξουσι
δὲ αἱ ἡδοναί, τὰ δὲ συναύξοντα οἰκεῖα.
        ARISTOTLE, *Eth. Nicom.* X. v. 2.

Tranio, having mentioned Aristotle's checks,
logic, rhetoric, music and poesy, mathematics
and metaphysics, says:

Fall to them as you find your stomach serves you :
No profit grows, where is no pleasure ta'en ;—
In brief, sir, study what you most affect.

And the reader will perceive that Aristotle in
his Ethics says, that those taking pleasure in
geometry become geometricians, and perceive
each thing better; and that those loving the
muses, &c., progress because they take pleasure
in the occupation.

Bastard. And why rail I on this Commodity ?
But for because he hath not woo'd me yet :
Not that I have the power to clutch my hand,
When his fair *angels* would *salute* my palm :
But for my hand, as unattempted yet,
Like a poor beggar, raileth on the rich.
Well, whiles I am a beggar, I will rail,
And say—there is no sin, but to be rich.
King John, Act ii. Sc. 1.

Our gold is either old or new. The old is that which
hath remained since the time of King Edward the Third,
or beene coined by such other princes as have reigned since
his decease, and without anie abasing or diminution of
the finesse of that mettall. Thereof also we have yet
remaining, the *riall*, the George noble, the Henrie *riall*,
the salut, the angell, and their small peeces as halfes, or
quarters, though these in my time are not so common
to be seene.—HOLINSHED, *The Description of England,*
Second Booke, cap. 25.

Salute, salus, was a coyn of gold stamped by King
Henry the Fifth in France, after his conquests there :

whereon the arms of England and France were stamped quarterly.—Stow's *Chron.* p. 589.

I think that Shakespeare plays upon the word salute in this passage, using it in a double sense in connection with the word angel, and I am able to quote a passage from Beaumont and Fletcher, in which the word salute is also played upon in a similar way:

Morecraft. My notable, dear friend, and worthy Master Loveless, and now right worshipful, all joy and welcome!

Young Loveless. Thanks to my dear incloser Master.

Morecraft. Pr'ythee, old *angel-gold, salute* my family, I'll do as much for yours.

> *The Scornful Lady*, Act ii. Sc. 3.

Young Loveless evidently plays upon the word salute, using it in connection with the word angel-gold: he also speaks of *old angel-gold*; and Holinshed, who wrote in Shakespeare's time, speaking of *old gold* coins, says, 'we have yet remaining, the riall, the George noble, the Henrie riall, the salut, the angell.'

Chief Justice. You follow the young prince up and down, like his ill angel.

Falstaff. Not so, my lord; your ill angel is light; but, I hope, he that looks upon me, will take me without weighing: and yet, in some respects, I grant, I cannot go: I cannot tell.

> 2 *Henry IV.*, Act i. Sc. 2.

Falstaff, referring to his great weight, says, in effect, 'I am not his ill angel, because your ill angel is light; but he that looks upon me, will take me without weighing.'

Although in 'King John' the word 'rail' is used immediately after the words salute and angel, it may be considered very doubtfnl whether Shakespeare there plays upon that word, although he often uses, in a double sense, words which do not differ more from each other in sound and meaning than the words 'rail' and 'rial.'

Proteus.   O, 'tis the curse in love, and still approved,
When women cannot love where they're beloved.
　　　　　　Two Gentlemen of Verona, Act v. Sc. 4.

Helena.   What though I be not so in grace as you,
So hung upon with love, so fortunate;
But *miserable most, to love unloved?*
This you should pity, rather than despise.
　　　　　　Midsummer Night's Dream, Act iii. Sc. 2.

ἐν δὲ τῇ ἐρωτικῇ ἐνίοτε μὲν ὁ ἐραστὴς ἐγκαλεῖ ὅτι ὑπερφιλῶν οὐκ ἀντιφιλεῖται.
　　　　　　ARISTOTLE, *Eth. Nicom.* IX. i. 2.

Χαλεπὸν τὸ μὴ φιλῆσαι·
Χαλεπὸν δὲ καὶ φιλῆσαι·

Χαλεπώτερον δὲ πάντων
'Αποτυγχάνειν φιλοῦντα.

ANACREON, *Od.* xlvi. Εἰς Ἔρωτα.

Shakespeare and Aristotle probably refer to this Ode of Anacreon.

Biron.   And among three, to love the worst of all.

Love's Labour's Lost, Act iii. Sc. 1.

And Biron may refer to the greatest of the three grievances in love mentioned by Anacreon, namely:

'Αποτυγχάνειν φιλοῦντα.

First Cap.   Nay, sit, nay, sit, good cousin Capulet;
For you and I are past our dancing days :
How long is 't now, since last yourself and I
Were in a mask ?
    Second Cap.   By 'r lady, thirty years.
    First Cap.   What, man! 'tis not so much, 'tis not so
       much :
'Tis since the nuptial of Lucentio,
Come Pentecost as quickly as it will,
Some five and twenty years ; and then we masked.
    Second Cap.   'Tis more, 'tis more, his son is elder, sir;
His son is thirty.
    First Cap.   Will you tell me that ?
His son was but a ward two years ago.

Romeo and Juliet, Act i. Sc. 5.

Tenure by homage, fealty, and escuage, is to hold by knight service, and it draweth to it ward marriage, and

relief. For when such tenant dieth, and his heir male be
within the age of twenty-one years, the lord shall have
the land holden of him until the age of the heir of twenty-
one years ; the which is called full age, because such
heir, by intendment of law, is not able to do such knight's
service before his age of twenty-one years. And also if
such heir be not married at the time of the death of his
ancestor, then the lord shall have the wardship and marriage of him.—LITTLETON's *Tenures*, Sec. 103. Wardship
was abolished by the 12th Car. II. cap. 24.

The first Capulet says it cannot be so much
as thirty years since they were in a mask at
the nuptial of Lucentio, but some five and
twenty years, because Lucentio's son was a ward
two years ago. The period of wardship lasted
until the ward attained twenty-one years of
age ; the two years since Lucentio's son was a
ward and twenty-one years make twenty-three
years. Thus, the age of Lucentio's son, according to the first Capulet's method of computa-
tion, was twenty-three years, and then the
ordinary period of gestation, and the period
between the time when the Capulets were
speaking and Pentecost, might make up 'some
five and twenty years.'

Hamlet. There is a play to-night before the king ;
One scene of it comes near the circumstance,
Which I have told thee of my father's death.
I pr'ythee, when thou seest that act afoot,
Even with the very comment of thy soul
Observe my uncle : if his *occulted* guilt
Do not itself unkennel in one speech,
It is a damned ghost that we have seen ;
And my imaginations are as foul
As Vulcan's stithy.   Act iii. Sc. 2.

All the ancient authors, of old time defined murder
to be *occulta* hominis occisio, &c., when it was done in
secret, so as the offender was not known ; but now it is
taken in a larger sense.—COKE, 3 *Instit.* cap. 7.

Hamlet, who knew how his father had been
poisoned by Claudius, speaks of his uncle's
occulted guilt, and Fleta says :

Traditores : qui alicui *occulte* venenum praebuerint
unde expiravit, et inde convincantur, detractentur et
suspendantur.—Lib. i. c. 35.

An ordinary is a handsome house, where every day,
about the hour of twelve, a good dinner is prepared
by way of ordinary, composed of variety of dishes, in
season, well drest, with all other accommodations fit for
that purpose; whereby many gentlemen of great estates
and good repute make this place their resort, who after
dinner play a while for recreation, both moderately and
commonly, without deserving reproof. But here is the
mischief : the best wheat will have tares growing amongst
it ; rooks and daws will sometimes be in the company
of pigeons ; nor can real gentlemen now-a-days so se-

cludo themselves from the society of such as are pre-
tendly so, but that they oftentimes mix company, being
much of the same colour and feather, and by the eye
undistinguishable.

The day being shut in, you may properly compare
this place to those countries which lye far in the North,
where it is as clear at midnight as at noonday; and
though it is a house of sin, yet you cannot call it a house
of darkness, for the candles never go out till morning,
unless the sudden fury of a losing gamester make them
extinct.

Pandarus. Why, he is very young: and yet will he,
within three pound, lift as much as his brother Hector.
Cressida. Is he so young a man, and so old a lifter?
Troilus and Cressida, Act i. Sc. 2.

This is the time (when ravenous beasts usually seek
for prey) wherein comes shoals of Huffs, *Hectors,* Setters,
Gilts, Pads, Biters, Divers, *Lifters,* Filers, Budgies,
Droppers, Crossbyters, &c., and these may all pass under
the general and common appellation of Rooks; and in
this particular, an ordinary serves as a nursery for
Tyburn: for if any one will put himself to the trouble
of observation, he shall find that there is seldom a year
wherein there are not some of this gang hung as pre-
cious jewels in the car of Tyburn. Look back and you
will find a great many gone already; God knows how
many are to follow.

Hectors and lifters, according to this old
author, passed under the general and common
appellation of rooks. Cressida evidently plays
upon the word 'lifter;' and it may be con-

sidered probable that Pandarus also uses the word 'hector' in a double sense.

These Rooks are in continual motion, walking from one table to another, till they can discover some unexperienced young gentleman, casheer or apprentice, that is come to this school of virtue, being unskilled in the quibbles and devices there practised; these they call Lambs, or Colls. Then do the Rooks (more properly called Wolves) strive who shall fasten on him first, following him close and engaging him in some advantageous Bets, and at length worries him, that is, gets all his money, and then the Rooks (Rogues I should have said) laugh and grin, saying, the Lamb is bitten.

Enobarbus. The itch of his affection should not then Have *nick'd* his captainship.
Antony and Cleopatra, Act iii. Sc. 6.

But that which will most provoke (in my opinion) any man's rage to a just satisfaction, is their throwing many times at a good sum with a dry fist (as they call it); that is, if they *nick* you, 'tis theirs; if they lose, they owe you so much, with many other quillets.

Perhaps the word *nick*, used by this old author, and by Shakespeare, in this passage, may be correctly derived from the Greek verb νικάω (νίκη), to conquer, to prevail over, to get the upper hand, &c.

If you *nick* them, 'tis odds if they wait not your coming out at night and beat you. I could produce you an hundred examples in this kind, but they will rarely adventure on the attempt, unless they are backt with some Bully-Huffs and Bully-Rooks, with others whose fortunes are as desperate as their own.

Falstaff. Mine host of the garter !

Host. What says my *bully-rook ?* speak scholarly and wisely.

Falstaff. Truly, mine host, I must turn away some of my followers.

Host. Discard, *bully Hercules* ; cashier : let them wag ; trot, trot.

Falstaff. I sit at ten pounds a week.

Host. Thou 'rt an emperor, Cæsar, Keisar, and Pheezar. I will entertain Bardolph ; he shall draw, he shall tap : said I well, *bully Hector ?*

Merry Wives of Windsor, Act i. Sc. 3.

Host. How now, *bully-rook ?* thou 'rt a gentleman : cavalero-justice, I say.

Shal. I follow, mine host, I follow.—Good even, and twenty, good master Page. Master Page, will you go with us ? we have sport in hand.

Host. Tell him, cavalero-justice ; tell him, *bully-rook.*

Shal. Sir, there is a fray to be fought between Sir Hugh the Welch priest, and Caius the French doctor.

Ford. Good mine host o' the Garter, a word with you.

Host. What sayest thou, *bully-rook ?*

Merry Wives of Windsor, Act ii. Sc. 2.

Host. I'll call.—*Bully knight ! Bully Sir John !* speak from thy lungs military : Art thou there ? it is thine host, thine Ephesian, calls.

Fal. (*Above.*) How now, mine host ?

Host. Here's a Bohemian Tartar tarries the coming down of thy fat woman : Let her descend, *bully,* let her descend ; my chambers are honourable.

Merry Wives of Windsor, Act iv. Sc. 5.

The more subtle and gentiler sort of Rooks you shall not distinguish by their outward demeanour from persons of condition; these will sit by a whole evening, and observe who wins; if the winner be bubbleable, they will insinuate themselves into his company by applauding his success, advising him to leave off whilst he is well; and lastly, by civilly inviting him to drink a glass of wine, where having well warm'd themselves to make him more than half drunk, they wheadle him into play; to which if he condescend he shall quickly have no money left him in his pocket, unless, perchance, a crown the Rooking-winner lent him in courtesie, to bear his charges homewards.

Pistol. Let vultures gripe thy guts! for gourd and fulham holds,
And *high* and *low* beguile the rich and poor.
Merry Wives of Windsor, Act i. Sc. 3.

This they do by false dice, as *High-Fullams* 4, 5, 6, *Low Fullams* 1, 2, 3. By Bristle-Dice, which are fitted for their purpose by sticking a hog's-bristle so in the corners, or otherwise in the dice, that they shall run high or low as they please; this bristle must be strong and short, by which means the bristle bending, it will not lie on that side, but will be tript over; and this is the newest way of making a high or low Fullam: the old ways are by drilling them, and loading them with quicksilver; but that cheat may be easily discovered by their weight, or holding two corners between your forefinger and thumb; if holding them so gently between your fingers they turn, you may then conclude them false; or you may try their falsehood otherwise, by breaking or splitting them: others have made them by filing and rounding; but all these ways fall short of the art of those who make them.

This description of an ordinary and its frequenters in the seventeenth century I have taken from an old book called, ' The Compleat Gamester, or Instructions how to play all manner of usual and most gentile Games,' &c.

Sir Nathaniel. Laus deo, bone intelligo.
Holofernes. Bone?—bone, for bene: Priscian a little scratch'd ; 'twill serve.

Love's Labour's Lost, Act v. Sc. 1.

Your next intollerable vice is solecismus, or incongruitie, as when we speak false English; that is, by misusing the grammaticall rules to be observed in cases, genders, tenses, and such like. Every poore scholler knowes the fault, and calls it the breaking of Priscian's head, for he was among the Latines a principall grammarian. — PUTTENHAM's *Arte of English Poesie,* lib. iii. chap. 22.

Puttenham evidently refers to Priscianus of Cæsarea, who lived probably in the sixth century. His grammatical commentaries, in eighteen books, form the most extensive ancient work on the grammar of the Latin language extant. The first sixteen books treat of the several parts of speech, and are commonly called the Larger Priscian, and the two last books treat of syntax, and are called the Smaller Priscian. Holofernes was a schoolmaster, and he probably refers to the fault which Puttenham calls 'the breaking of Priscian's head.'

Val. Now, trust me, madam, it came hardly off;
For, being ignorant to whom it goes,
I writ at random, very *doubtfully.*
    Sil. Perchance you think too much of so much
        pains ?
    Val. No, madam ; so it stead you, I will write,
Please you command, a thousand times as much :
And yet—
    Sil. A pretty period! Well, I guess the sequel ;
And *yet* I will not name it : and *yet* I care not ;
And *yet* take this again : and *yet* I thank you ;
Meaning henceforth to trouble you no more.
    Speed. And *yet* you will ; and *yet* another yet.
          Two Gentlemen of Verona, Act ii. Sc. 1.

    Hamlet. Here, as before, never, so help you mercy,
How strange or odd soe'er I bear myself,
As I perchance hereafter shall think meet
To put an antic disposition on,
That you, at such times seeing me, never shall,
With arms encumber'd thus, or this head-shake,
Or by pronouncing of some *doubtful* phrase,
As 'Well, well, we know,' or 'We could, an if we
       would,'
Or 'If we list to speak,' or 'There be, an if they might,'
Or such ambiguous giving out, to note
That you know aught of me.
                    Act i. Sc. 5.

Not much unlike the wondrer have ye another figure, called the *doublfull*, because oftentimes we will seeme to cast perils, and make doubt of things, when by a plaine manner of speech we might affirme or deny him, as thus of a cruell mother who murdred her owne child :

Whether the cruell mother were more to blame,
Or the shrewd childe come of so curst a dame ;
Or whether some smatch of the father's blood,
Whose kinne were never kinde, nor never good,
Mooved her thereto, &c.'
        The Arte of English Poesie, Lib. iii. Chap. 19.

Queen Margaret.   Butchers and villains, bloody canni-
bals !
How sweet a plant have you untimely cropp'd !
You have no children, butchers ! if you had,
The thought of them would have stirr'd up remorse !
        3 *Henry VI.*, Act v. Sc. 5.

Macd.   My children too ?
Rosse.   Wife, children, servants, all
That could be found.
Macd.   And I must be from thence !
My wife kill'd too ?
Rosse.   I have said.
Mal.   Be comforted :
Let's make us med'cines of our great revenge,
To cure this deadly grief.
Macd. He has no children.
        Macbeth, Act iv. Sc. 3.

πρόσπιπτε δ' οἰκτρῶς τοῦδ' Ὀδυσσέως γόνυ.
καὶ πεῖθ'. ἔχεις δὲ πρόφασιν· ἐστι γὰρ τέκνα
καὶ τῷδε, τὴν σὴν ὥστ' ἐποικτεῖραι τύχην. 341.
        EURIPIDES, EKABH.

Hostess. A' made a finer end and went away an it had been any *christom* child.

Henry V., Act ii. Sc. 3.

Here is to be noted, as for the intent of things aforesaid, as for those that follow, the which in this solemnity of exorcism, or of conjuration of the devil; some things they make in operation without all only, the which things are not in the soul materially. But they betoken things spiritual, as in putting the salt in the mouth of the child, the putting of the spittle of the priest in his nostrils and in his ears, he making the cross with the holy oil in the breast and between the shoulders. Also, after the baptism, he maketh the cross with the holy creme upon the child's head; he putteth on him afterwards the white robe, the which is called the *crysome.* —*The Ordynarye of Crysten Men.* Enprynted in the Cyte of London, in the Fleete Strete, in the sygne of ye Sonne, by Wynkynde de Worde, ye yere of our lord MCCCCVJ.

Sicinius.   It is a mind,
That shall remain a poison where it is,
Not poison any farther.
  Coriolanus.   Shall remain!—
Hear you this Triton of the minnows? mark you
His absolute *shall?*
  Cominius.   'Twas from the canon.
  Coriolanus.   Shall
O good, but most unwise patricians! why,
You grave, but reckless senators, have you thus
Given Hydra here to choose an officer,
That with his peremptory *shall*, being but
The horn and noise o' the monsters, wants not spirit
To say, he'll turn your current in a ditch,
And make your channel his?

Coriolanus, Act iii. Sc. 1.

The contrast between Triton, the son of Neptune and Amphitrite, and the minnows, which are very small fish, is apparent ; and, although it may be truly said that Triton, as a deity of the sea, would rule over the minnows with his 'absolute' or 'peremptory' shall, which Coriolanus calls 'the horn and noise o' the monster,' yet, when it is remembered that Triton used to announce the approach of Neptune by blowing his horn, which was a large conch, or sea-shell, it may be considered probable that Shakespeare plays upon the word 'shall' in this passage, using it in a double sense; for the words 'shall' and 'shell' do not differ more from each other in sound than the words 'sheep' and 'ship,' which Speed plays upon in the 'Two Gentlemen of Verona,' Act i. Sc. 1; and it may also be considered probable that Shakespeare, further on in the same passage, plays upon the word *shall*, using it again in a double sense :

> They choose their magistrate ;
> And such a one as he, who puts his *shall*,
> His popular *shall*, against a graver bench
> Than ever frown'd in Greece !

For the reader will perceive that Coriolanus speaks of 'such a one as he, who puts his *shall*

against a graver bench than ever frown'd in
Greece;' and Shakespeare, using the word *shall*
in a double sense, may refer to the practice in
ancient Greece of banishing persons considered
dangerous to the state by ostracism, ὀστρακισμός,
where the votes were given by shells, ὄστρακα,
each man marking upon his ὄστρακον, or *his
shell*, the name of the person he would have
banished.

Silius.   Noble Ventidius,
Whilst yet with Parthian *blood thy sword is warm*,
The fugitive Parthians follow.
                    Antony and Cleopatra, Act iii. Sc. 1.

                        ἀλλά οἱ αὖθι
λῦσε μένος, πλῆξας ξίφει αὐχένα κωπήεντι.
πᾶν δ᾽ ὑπεθερμάνθη ξίφος αἵματι. 331.
                    HOMER, ΙΛΙΑΔΟΣ Π'.

        ὁ δ᾽ ᾽Αγήνορος υἱὸν ῞Εχεκλον
μέσσην κακκεφαλὴν ξίφει ἤλασε κωπήεντι.
πᾶν δ᾽ ὑπεθερμάνθη ξίφος αἵματι. 476.
                    HOMER, ΙΛΙΑΔΟΣ Υ'.

Touch.   Nay, if I keep not my *rank*—
Ros.   Thou losest thy *old smell*.
                    As You Like It, Act i. Sc. 2.

Certes the making of new gentlemen bred great
strife sometimes amongst the Romans; I meane when
those which were Novi homines were more allowed of
for their vertues newlie scene and shewed, than the *old
smell of ancient race* latelie defaced by the cowardise and

evill life of their nephues and defendants could make the
others to be.—HOLINSHED, *The Description of England*,
chap. 5.

Nurse. I saw the wound, *I saw it with mine eyes,*—
God save the mark!—here on his manly breast.
Romeo and Juliet, Act iii. Sc. 2.

Fal. Pistol!—
Pist. *He hears with ears.*
Eva. The tevil and his tam! what phrase is this,
He hears with ear? Why, it is affectations.
Fal. Pistol, did you pick master Slender's purse?
Merry Wives of Windsor, Act i. Sc. 1.

Shakespeare, in these passages, probably refers to 'the vice of surplusage,' thus described
by Puttenham:—

Also the poet or maker's speech becomes viscious
and unpleasant by nothing more than by using too much
surplusage: and this lieth not only in a word or two
more than ordinary, but in whole clauses, and perad-
venture large sentences impertinently spoken, or with
more labour and curiositie than is requisite. The first
surplusage the Greekes call Pleonasmus, I call him too
full speech and is no great fault, as if one should say,
I heard it with mine ears, and saw it with mine eyes, as if
a man could heare with his heeles or see with his nose.
We ourselves used this superfluous speech in a verse
written of our mistresse, nevertheles, not much to be
misliked, for even a vice sometime being seasonably
used, hath a pretie grace:

For ever may my true love live and never die,
And that mine eyes may see her crownde a Queene.

As, if she lived ever, she could ever die, or that one
might see her crowned without eyes.—*The Arte of
English Poesie*, Lib. iii. chap. 22.

Horatio.   A mote it is to trouble the mind's eye.
In the most high and palmy state of Rome,
A little ere the mightiest Julius fell,
The graves stood tenantless, and the sheeted dead
Did squeak and gibber in the Roman streets:
As stars with trains of fire and *dews of blood*,
Disasters in the sun; and the moist star
Upon whose influence Neptune's empire stands
Was sick almost to doomsday with eclipse:
And even the like precurse of fierce events,
As harbingers preceding still the fates
And prologue to the omen coming on,
Have heaven and earth together demonstrated
Unto our climatures and countrymen.
                              Hamlet, Act i. Sc. 1.

ἱππῆες δ' ὀλίγον μετεκίαθον· ἐν δὲ κυδοιμὸν
ὦρσε κακὸν Κρονίδης, κατὰ δ' ὑψόθεν ἧκεν ἐέρσας
αἵματι μυδαλέας ἐξ αἰθέρος.   54.
                              HOMER, ΙΛΙΑΔΟΣ Λ΄.

Calphurnia.   Fierce fiery warriors fight upon the
        clouds,
In ranks, and squadrons, and right form of war,
Which *drizzled blood* upon the Capitol.
                              Julius Cæsar, Act ii. Sc. 2.

Sæpe inter nimbos guttæ cecidere cruentæ.
                              OVID, *Met.* xv. 788

In the furthermost parts of Scotland it *rained blood*.
HOLINSHED, *The Historie of Scotland*.

2nd Thief. I'll believe him as an enemy, and give over my trade.

Timon of Athens, Act iv. Sc. 3.

Duke. I know thee well: How dost thou, my good fellow?

Clo. Truly, sir, the better for my foes, and the worse for my friends.

Duke. Just the contrary; the better for thy friends.

Clo. No, sir, the worse.

Duke. How can that be?

Clo. Marry, sir, they praise me, and make an ass of me; now, my foes tell me plainly I am an ass: so that by my foes, sir, I profit in the knowledge of myself, and by my friends I am abused: so that, conclusions to be as kisses, if your four negatives make your two affirmatives, why then, the worse for my friends, and the better for my foes.

Twelfth Night, Act v. Sc. 1.

That we may learn many things from our enemies is a sentiment to be found in one of the comedies of Aristophanes:

ΕΠΟΨ.

εἰ δὲ τὴν φύσιν μὲν ἐχθροί, τὸν δὲ νοῦν εἰσιν φίλοι,
καὶ διδάξοντές τι δεῦρ' ἥκουσιν ὑμᾶς χρήσιμον;

ΧΟΡΟΣ.

πῶς δ' ἂν οἶδ' ἡμᾶς τι χρήσιμον διδάξειάν ποτε,
ἢ φράσειαν, οἵτες ἐχθροὶ τοῖσι πάπποις τοῖς ἐμοῖς;

c 3

ΕΠΟΨ.

ἀλλ' ἀπ' ἐχθρῶν δῆτα πολλὰ μανθάνουσιν οἱ σοφοί.
ἡ γὰρ εὐλάβεια σώζει πάντα· παρὰ μὲν οὖν φίλου
οὐ μάθοις ἂν τοῦθ'· ὁ δ' ἐχθρὸς εὐθὺς ἐξηνάγκασεν.
αὐτίχ' αἱ πόλεις παρ' ἀνδρῶν γ' ἔμαθον ἐχθρῶν, κοὐ φίλων,
ἐκπονεῖν θ' ὑψηλὰ τείχη ναῦς τε κεκτῆσθαι μακράς.
τὸ δὲ μάθημα τοῦτο σώζει παῖδας, οἶκον, χρήματα.

ΧΟΡΟΣ.

ἐστι μὲν λόγων ἀκοῦσαι πρῶτον, ὡς ἡμῖν δοκεῖ,
χρήσιμον· μάθοι γὰρ ἄν τις κἀπὸ τῶν ἐχθρῶν σοφόν. 382.

ARISTOPHANES, ΟΡΝΙΘΕΣ.

Cade. Nay, answer if you can: The Frenchmen are
our enemies: go to then, I ask but this: Can he, that
speaks with the tongue of an enemy, be a good counsellor, or no?

All. No, no; and therefore we'll have his head.

2 *Henry VI.*, Act iv. Sc. 2.

To use the language of Stafford, the 'gross
and miserable ignorance' of Cade's followers
makes them decide that no man that speaks
with the tongue of an enemy can be a good
counsellor.

Beat. By my troth, I am sick.

Mary. Get you some of this distilled Carduus Benedictus, and lay it to your heart; it is the only thing for
a qualm.

Hero. There thou prick'st her with a thistle.

Beat. Benedictus! why Benedictus? you have some
moral in this Benedictus.

Mary. Moral? no, by my troth, I have no moral
meaning; I meant, plain holy-thistle.

Much Ado about Nothing, Act iii. Sc. 4.

We entend to begin with that worthie hearbe named the *blessed thistle* (for his singular vertues) as well against poysons, as the pestilent ague, and other perillous diseases of the heart: which to many at this day is very well knowne, although great controversies have beene amongst the ancient phisitions, about the true description of the hearbe: for both the name and forme of the hearbe, doe declare the same to be a kind of thistle: yet the learned Ruellius, writing of the blessed Thistle, came nearer to a troth, and faithfuller described the forme of the hearbe: in that he affirmed the same to have a big stalke, and leaves crisped with prickles (after the condition of the Endive), the flowre yellowish, and seedes small, contained within the soft downe (as in the other Thistles), and that they do late waxe ripe.'—*The Gardener's Labyrinth.*

To understand this passage in 'Much Ado about Nothing,' I think it will be necessary to suppose that Margaret, who knows that Beatrice loves Benedict, uses the Latin name of the holy-thistle, Carduus Benedictus, because it includes the sound and also the letters of the name 'Benedict.' Margaret plays upon the word Benedictus, and uses it, or at least a part of it, in a double sense, and Beatrice evidently suspects a double meaning, because she says, 'Benedictus! why Benedictus? you have some moral in this Benedictus.'

The blessed thistle, according to 'The Gardener's Labyrinth,' was considered to have 'singular virtue' against 'perillous diseases of

the heart.' Beatrice was in love with Benedict; she had an affection of the heart, and
Margaret, speaking of the blessed thistle, says
to her, 'lay it to your heart.'

Lear. I have seen the day, with my good biting
falchion
I would have made them skip: I am old now,
And these same crosses spoil me.

Act v. Sc. 3.

Othello. I have seen the day,
That with this little arm and this good sword
I have made my way through more impediments
Than twenty times your stop.

Act v. Sc. 2.

Page. I have heard the Frenchman hath good skill
in his rapier.

Shal. Tut, sir! I could have told you more: in these
times you stand on distance, your passes, stoccadoes,
and I know not what: 'tis the heart, master Page; 'tis
here, 'tis here. I have seen the time, with my long
sword, I would have made you four tall fellows skip
like rats.

Merry Wives of Windsor, Act ii. Sc. 1.

ῥώμη γὰρ ἐκλέλοιπεν ἣν πρὶν εἴχομεν·
γήρᾳ δὲ τρομερὰ γυῖα κἀμαυρὸν σθένος.
εἰ δ᾽ ἦν νέος τε κἄτι σώματος κρατῶν,
λαβὼν ἂν ἔγχος τοῦδε τοὺς ξανθοὺς πλόκους
καθημάτωσ᾽ ἄν, ὥστ᾽ Ἀτλαντικῶν πέρα
φεύγειν ὅρων ἂν δειλίᾳ τοὐμὸν δόρυ. 235.

EURIPIDES, ΗΡΑΚΛΗΣ ΜΑΙΝΟΜΕΝΟΣ.

Amphitryon, Lear, Othello, and Shallow, all
speak of what they would have done, had they
not been old.

Host. By this heavenly ground I tread on, I must be fain to pawn both my plate, and the tapestry of my dining-chambers.

Fal. Glasses, glasses, is the only drinking.

   *   *   *   *   *   *

Host. Pray thee, Sir John, let it be but twenty nobles: i' faith I am loath to pawn my plate, in good earnest, la.   2 *Henry IV.*, Act ii. Sc. i.

It is a world to see in these our days, wherein gold and silver most aboundeth, how that our gentilitie, as loathing those mettals (because of the plentie), do now generallie choose rather the Venice *glasses* both for our wine and beere, than anie of those mettals or stone wherein before time we have beene accustomed to drinke, but such is the nature of man generallie, that he most coveteth things difficult to be atteined ; and such is the estimation of this stuffe, that manie become rich onelie with their new trade unto Murana (a towne neere to Venice, situat on the Adriatike sea), from whence the verie best are dailie to be had, and such as for beautie do well neere match the christall, or the ancient Murrhina vasa, whereof now no man hath knowledge.   And as this is scene in the gentilitie, so in the wealthie communalitie the like desire of glasse is not neglected, whereby the gaine gotten by their purchase is yet much more increased, to the benefit of the merchant.   The poorest also will have glasse if they may, but sith the Venecian is somewhat too deere for them, they content themselves with such as are made at home of ferne and burned stone, but in fine all go one waie, that is to *shards* at last, so that our great expenses in glasses (beside that they breed much strife toward such as have the charge of them) are worst of all bestowed in mine opinion, because their peeces do turn to no profit.—HOLINSHED, *The Description of England.*

First Priest.   Her obsequies have been as far enlarged
As we have warrantise : her death was doubtful,
And, but that great command o'ersways the order,
She should in ground unsanctified have lodged
Till the last trumpet ; for charitable prayers,
Shards, flints, and pebbles should be thrown on her :
Yet here she is allow'd her virgin crants,
Her maiden strewments and the bringing home
Of bell and burial.

Hamlet, Act v. Sc. 1.

I think the glasses mentioned by Falstaff
are the Venice glasses which Holinshed here
speaks of. The Hostess says, ' I must be fain to
pawn my plate,' &c.; but Falstaff makes this
consolatory answer, ' Glasses, glasses, is the
only drinking;' and Holinshed, who wrote in
Shakespeare's time, says :

In these our days, wherein gold and silver most aboundeth, our gentilitie, as loathing those mettals (because of
their plentie), do now generallie choose rather Venice
glasses both for our wine and beere.

Weary with toil, I haste me to my bed,
    The dear repose for limbs with travel tired ;
But then begins a journey in my head,
    To work my mind, when body's works expired.

Sonnet xxvii.

ἤματα μὲν γὰρ τέρπομ' ὀδυρομένη, γοόωσα,
ἔς τ' ἐμὰ ἔργ' ὁρόωσα καὶ ἀμφιπόλων ἐνὶ οἴκῳ·
αὐτὰρ ἐπὴν νὺξ ἔλθῃ, ἕλῃσί τε κοῖτος ἅπαντας,

κεῖμαι ἐνὶ λέκτρῳ, πυκιναὶ δέ μοι ἀμφ᾽ ἁδινὸν κῆρ
ὀξεῖαι μελεδῶναι ὀδυρομένην ἐρέθουσιν. 519.

ΠΟΜΕΡ. ΟΔΥΣΣΕΙΑΣ Τ΄.

Queen.   O, I am press'd to death,
Through want of speaking!
Richard II., Act iii. Sc. 4.

Pandarus. Amen. Whereupon I will show you a
chamber with a bed : which bed, because it shall not
speak of your pretty encounters, press it to death : away!
—*Troilus and Cressida*, Act iii. Sc. 2.

Shakespeare in these passages probably refers
to *peine forte et dure*, a punishment inflicted on
those who, being arraigned of felony, and re-
fusing to put themselves upon the ordinary
trial of ' God and the country,' were by the
interpretation of law considered to be mute.
This *peine forte et dure* was vulgarly called
pressing to death.

The judgment [says Coke] is that the man or woman
shall be remanded to the prison, and laid there in some
low and dark house, where they shall lie naked on the
bare earth without any litter, rushes, or other clothing,
and without any garment about them, and that they shall
lie upon their backs, their heads uncovered and their
feet, and one arm shall be drawn to one quarter of the
house with a cord, and the other arm to another quarter,
and in the same manner shall be done with their legs,
and there shall be laid upon their bodies iron and stone,
so much as they may bear, and more, and the next day
following they shall have three morsels of barley bread
without any drink, and the second day they shall drink

thrice of the water that is next to the house of the prison
(except running water) without any bread, and this
shall be their diet until they be dead.—2. *Inst.* 178.

Wood, in his 'Institute' (second edition, page
633), says:

If one arraigned of Petit Treason or Felony stands
mute, or answers nothing at all, it shall be enquired
whether he stands mute on purpose, or whether he is
dumb. If he stands mute out of stubbornness, or if he
hath cut out his tongue, or he does not plead directly, or
does not put himself upon a trial by the country if a
commoner, or if a peer by God and his peers, after he
has pleaded not guilty, he shall be put to the penance
peine forte et dure, with forfeiture of goods. But before
the judgment passes the Court orders his thumbs to be
tied together with whipcord, and to be drawn together
by the whole strength of two men, to give the criminal
a taste of his pain to be endured, if he will not then
comply. This [continues Wood] is the practice at New-
gate Sessions.

This punishment was common long before,
during, and after Shakespeare's time, and it is
reasonable to suppose that any allusion to
'pressing to death' would be well understood
by the audiences of the 'Globe.' The Queen
and Pandarus seem to refer not only to this
punishment, but also to its cause—namely, 're-
fusing to speak,' or 'standing mute,' or, to use
the Queen's own words, 'want of speaking.'

Westmoreland. There is no need of any such redress ;
Or, if there were, it *not belongs* to you.
  *   *   *   *   *   *
Yet, for your part it *not appears* to me.
      2 *Henry IV.*, Act iv. Sc. 1.

Prospero. Ye elves of hills, brooks, standing lakes,
  and groves ;
And ye, that on the sands with printless foot
Do chase the ebbing Neptune, and do fly him
When he comes back ; you demi-puppets, that
By moonshine do the green-sour ringlets make,
Whereof the ewe *not bites.*   *Tempest,* Act v. Sc. 1.

Your misplacing and preposterous placing is not all
one in behaviour of language, for the misplacing is
alw. ies intollerable, but the preposterous is a pardonable
fault, and many times gives a pretie grace unto the
speech. We call it by a common saying, to set the cart
before the horse, and it may be done, eyther by a single
word or by a clause of speech. By a single word thus :

And if I *not performe,* God let me never thrive ;

for performe not : and this vice is sometimes tollerable
inough, but if the word carry any notable sence, it is a
vice not tollerable, as he that said, prasing a woman for
her red lippes, thus :

   A corall lippe of hew.

Which is no good speech, because either he should have
sayd no more but a corrall lip, which had bene inough
to declare the rednesse, or els he should have said, a lip
of corrall hew, and not a corall lip of hew. Now if this
disorder be in a whole clause which carieth more sentence
then a word, it is then worst of all.—PUTTENHAM, *The
Arte of English Poesie,* Lib. iii. Chap. 22.*

---

* *Not enriches,* Othello, Act iii. Sc. 3. *Not respects,* Cymbeline,
Act i. Sc. 7.

O, how her eyes and tears did lend and borrow!
Her eyes seen in the tears, tears in her eye;
Both crystals, where they view'd each other's *sorrow*,
Sorrow that friendly sighs sought still to dry;
But like a stormy day, now wind, now rain,
Sighs dry her cheeks, tears make them wet again.
Venus and Adonis, clxi.

His drumming heart cheers up his burning eye,
His eye commends the leading to *his hand*;
His hand, as proud of such a dignity,
Smoking with pride, march'd on to make his stand
On her bare breast, the heart of all her land:
Whose ranks of blue veins, as his hand did scale,
Left their round turrets destitute and pale.
Lucrece, lxiii.

Ye have another sort of repetition when with the
worde by which you finish your verse, ye beginne the
next verse with the same, as thus:

Comforte it is for man to have a *wife*,
Wife chast, and wise, and lowly all her life.

Or thus:

Your beutie was the cause of my first *love*,
Love while I live, that I may sore repent.

The Greeks call this figure Anadiplosis; I call him the
Redouble, as the originall beares.—PUTTENHAM, *The Arte
of English Poesie*, Lib. iii. Chap. 19.

In these passages, Shakespeare with the
word with which he finishes a verse, begins
the next.

Mrs. Ford. Nay, by the mass, that he did not; he
beat him most unpitifully, methought.

Mrs. Page. I'll have the cudgel hallowed, and hung o'er the altar ; it hath done meritorious service.

Merry Wives, Act iv. Sc. 2.

2nd Clown. Who builds stronger than a mason, a shipwright, or a carpenter ?

1st Clown. Ay, tell me that, and unyoke.

2nd Clown. Marry, now I can tell.

1st Clown. To 't.

2nd Clown. Mass, I cannot tell.

1st Clown. Cudgel thy brains no more about it ; for your dull ass will not mend his pace with beating.

Hamlet, Act v. Sc. 1.

Cudgel: derived from theWelsh *cogel*; from *côg*, a mass, lump, or short piece of wood. Mass: derived from the Saxon *maesa, maesse*; French *messe*; German and Danish *messe*. The word mass so derived signifies primarily leisure, or rest from labour: now, the service of the Romish Church; the office or prayers used at the celebration of the eucharist; the consecration of the bread and wine. Mass derived from the French *masse* signifies a mass, heap, a mace or club. Portuguese *maça*, dough and mace ; Spanish *masa*, dough, mortar, a mass, and *maza*, a club, a mace; *mazo*, a mallet; Italian *massa*, a heap, and *mazza*, a maze. These words are supposed to belong to the root of the Greek μάσσω, to

beat or pound, the root of which is μαγ: hence
the connection between mass and mace, a club.

Shakespeare, in these passages, may play
upon the words mass and cudgel, using them
in connection with each other: because the
word *cogel*, from which cudgel is derived, signifies a mass or lump. Thus, cudgel suggested
the meaning of the word from which it is derived, namely, 'mass' or lump; and this word
'mass,' which is the meaning of *cogel*, suggested
the Mass by which men swore.

Cominius.   I tell you, he does sit in gold, his eye
Red as 'twould burn Rome; and his injury
The gaoler to his pity.
Coriolanus, Act v. Sc. 1.

Coriolanus.   I sometime lay here in Corioli,
At a poor man's house; he used me kindly:
He cried to me; I saw him prisoner;
But then Aufidius was within my view,
And wrath o'erwhelm'd my pity.
Act i. Sc. 9.

Duke.   Merchant of Syracusa, plead no more;
I am not partial to infringe our laws:
The enmity and discord, which of late
Sprung from the rancorous outrage of your duke
To merchants, our well-dealing countrymen, —
Who, wanting gilders to redeem their lives,
Have seal'd his rigorous statutes with their bloods,—
Excludes all pity from our threat'ning looks.
Comedy of Errors, Act i. Sc. 1.

Καὶ μήτε ἐν ἀνδρείας πάθει ὄντες· οἷον ἐν ὀργῇ, ἢ θάρρει. ἀλόγιστα γὰρ τοῦ ἐσομένου ταῦτα· μήτ᾽ ἐν ὑβριστικῇ δια- θέσει· καὶ γὰρ οὗτοι ἀλόγιστοι τοῦ πείσεσθαί τι· ἀλλ᾽ οἱ μεταξὺ τούτων· μήτ᾽ αὖ φοβούμενοι σφόδρα, οὐ γὰρ ἐλεοῦσιν οἱ ἐκ- πεπληγμένοι διὰ τὸ εἶναι πρὸς τῷ οἰκείῳ πάθει. 7.

Albany. Produce their bodies, be they alive or dead!—
This judgment of the heavens, that makes us tremble,
Touches us not with pity.

Lear, Act v. Sc. 3.

Τὸ γὰρ δεινὸν ἕτερον τοῦ ἐλεεινοῦ καὶ ἐκκρουστικόν, καὶ πολλάκις τῷ ἐναντίῳ χρήσιμον. 13.

ARISTOTLE, ΤΕΧΝΗΣ ΡΗΤΟΡΙΚΗΣ κεφ. η'. Lib. ii.

Aristotle says that those who are in anger (ἐν ὀργῇ) do not feel pity, and Shakespeare says almost as much; for Cominius, speaking of Coriolanus, says, 'his injury is the gaoler to his pity,' and Coriolanus says,

'Wrath o'erwhelm'd my pity;'

so that the injury and wrath of Coriolanus, and the enmity mentioned by Ægeon, may be considered productive of or equivalent to the anger, or violent emotion or passion, mentioned by Aristotle.

King. What wouldst thou beg, Laertes,
That shall not be my offer, not thy asking?
The head is not more native to the heart,
The hand more instrumental to the mouth,
Than is the throne of Denmark to thy father.

Hamlet, Act i. Sc. 2.

Hor.   Is it a custom?

Ham. Ay, marry, is 't:
But to my mind,—though I am native here,
And to the manner born,—it is a custom
More honour'd in the breach than the observance.
This heavy-headed revel, east and west,
Makes us traduced, and tax'd of other nations.
                                Hamlet, Act i. Sc. 4.

Servi anciently signified bondsmen or servile
tenants. They were called 'servi, quia serva-
bantur à dominiis et non occidebantur, et non
à serviendo;' for the life and members of them,
as of freemen, were in the hands and pro-
tection of kings; and it was, in consequence of
the cruelty of some lords, ordained that he who
killed his villein should have the same judgment as if he had killed a freeman.   The
proper *servi* were of four sorts: the first, such
as sold themselves for a livelihood; the second,
debtors who were sold for payment of their
debts; the third, captives made in war, who
were maintained and employed as slaves; the
fourth, *nativi*, such as were the children of
villeins born in servitude within a particular
district or manor, and were by descent the sole
property of the lord.   About the year 1554,
Henry the Eighth manumitted two of his
villeins in these words:

" Whereas God created all men free, but afterwards
the laws and customs of nations subjected some under
the yoke of servitude, we think it pious and meritorious
with God to manumit Henry Knight, a taylor, and John
Herle, a husbandman, our *natives*, as being *born within
the manor* of Stoke Clymmysland, in our County of
Cornwall, together with all their goods, lands, and chat-
tels acquired or to be acquired, so as the said persons
and their issue shall from henceforth by us be free, and
of free condition."—*Barr. Stats.* 276.

The reader will perceive that Hamlet says:

> I am native here,
> And to the manner born ;

and also that in this form of enfranchisement
the King manumits ' Henry Knight and John
Herle, our natives, as being born within the
manor of Stoke Clymmysland.'

Hamlet may speak of Denmark or Elsinore
as the manor, himself as *nativus*, to the manor
born, and the ' heavy-headed revel ' as a custom incident to the manor.   In this passage
Shakespeare probably uses the word manor in
a double sense, as in *Love's Labour's Lost*,
Act i. Scene 1, where it is contrasted with the
word manner, and played upon:

Clown. I was scene with her in the mannor-house,
sitting with her upon the forme, and taken following her
into the parke : which put together is in manner and
form following.

If it should be considered probable that Hamlet uses the word manner in a double sense, it will then be of little consequence whether the word is spelt with 'e' or 'o,' because the mention of the one word would be intended to suggest to the mind the other word, which is *idem sonans*, but different in meaning.

Doll.   Why does the prince love him so, then ?
Falstaff.   Because their legs are both of a bigness : and he plays at quoits well, and eats conger and fennel ; and drinks off candles' ends for flap-dragons ; and rides the wild mare with the boys.

2 *Henry IV.*, Act ii. Sc. 4.

With that bestriding the mast, I gat by little and little towards him, after such manner as boyes are wont, when they ride the wilde mare.—*Arcadia*, Lib. ii. p. 192.

Constance.   Lame, foolish, crooked, swart, prodigious.

King John, Act iii. Sc. 1.

Enobarbus.   But he loves Cæsar best ;—Yet he loves
       Antony :
Ho ! hearts, tongues, figures, scribes, bards, poets cannot
Think, speak, cast, write, sing, number, ho, his love
To Antony.

Antony and Cleopatra, Act iii. Sc. 1.

Lady Capulet.   Accursed, unhappy, wretched, hateful day !
       *   *   *   *   *   *

Paris.   Beguiled, divorced, wronged, spited, slain !
       *   *   *   *   *   *

Capulet. Despised, distressed, hated, martyr'd, kill'd!
* * * * * *

     Romeo and Juliet, Act iv. Sc. 5.

Malcolm. But I have none : The king-becoming graces,
As justice, verity, temperance, stableness,
Bounty, perseverance, mercy, lowliness,
Devotion, patience, courage, fortitude,
I have no relish of them.

      Macbeth, Act iv. Sc. 3.

We use sometimes to proceede all by single words,
without any close or coupling, saving that a little pause
or comma is geven to every word. This figure for pleasure may be called in our vulgar the cutted comma, for
that there cannot be a shorter division then at every
word's end. The Greekes in their language call it short
language, as thus:

  Envy, malice, flattery, disdaine,
  Avarice, deceit, falshed, filthy gaine.

If this loose language be used, not in single words,
but in long clauses, it is called Asindeton. and in both
cases we utter in that fashion when either we be earnest,
or would seeme to make hast.—PUTTENHAM, *The Arte of
English Poesie*, Lib. iii. Chap. 19.

Shakespeare frequently uses this figure. and
in the few passages I have selected the reader
will perceive that some of the verses. to use
Puttenham's language, ' proceede all by single
words, without close or coupling, saving that
a little pause or comma is given to every
word,' thus:

  Accursed, unhappy, wretched. hateful day

       D

It may be said that Shakespeare does not use this figure in this passage, because Lady Capulet does not proceed entirely by single words, for a comma does not separate the adjective 'hateful' from the noun 'day'; but in the last line which Puttenham uses in illustration of the cutted comma, the adjective 'filthy' is not separated by a comma from the noun 'gain.'

———

Prince Henry. Charge an honest woman with picking thy pocket! Why, thou whoreson, impudent, embossed rascal, if there were anything in thy pocket but tavern-reckonings, memorandums of bawdy-houses, and one poor penny-worth of *sugar-candy to make thee long-winded*; if thy pocket were enriched with any other injuries but these, I am a villain.—1 *Henry IV.*, Act iii. Sc. 3.

According to 'The Compleat Gamester,' sugar-candy was, with other things, given to fighting cocks, to make them long-winded; for the author of that old book, in his instructions for 'dieting and ordering a cock for battel,' says:

You must put them in deep straw-baskets, made for the purpose, or for want of them take a couple of cock-ing-bags, and fill these with straw half-ways, then put in your cocks severally, and cover them over with straw to the top, then shut down the lids and let them sweat; but do not forget to give them first some white *sugar-*

candy, chopt rosemary, and butter mingled and incorpo-
rated together. Let the quantity be about the bigness
of a walnut. By so doing you will cleanse him of his
grease, increase his strength, and *prolong his breath*.

Gon. I' the commonwealth I would by contraries
Execute all things; for no kind of traffic
Would I admit; no name of magistrate;
Letters should not be known; riches, poverty,
And use of service, none; contract, succession,
Bourn, bound of land, tilth, vineyard, none;
No use of metal, corn, or wine, or oil;
No occupation; all men idle, all;
And women too, but innocent and pure;
No sovereignty—
   Seb.   Yet he would be king on 't.
   Ant. The latter end of his commonwealth forgets the
beginning.
   Gon. All things in common nature should produce
Without sweat or endeavour: treason, felony,
Sword, pike, knife, gun, or need of any engine,
Would I not have; but nature should bring forth,
Of its own kind, all foison, all abundance,
To feed my innocent people.
   Seb. No marrying 'mong his subjects?
   Ant. None, man; all idle: whores and knaves.
   Gon. I would with such perfection govern, sir,
To excel the golden age.
   Seb.   God save his majesty!
                   Tempest, Act ii. Sc. 1.

Cade. Be brave, then; for your captain is brave, and
vows reformation. There shall be in England seven
halfpenny loaves sold for a penny: the three-hooped pot
shall have ten hoops; and I will make it felony to drink
small beer: all the realm shall be in common; and in

Cheapside shall my palfry go to grass : and when I am
king, as king I will be—

All. God save your majesty !

Cade. I thank you, good people : there shall be no
money ; all shall eat and drink on my score ; and I will
apparel them all in one livery, that they may agree like
brothers and worship me their lord.

2 *Henry VI.*, Act iv. Sc. 2.

ΠΡΑΞΑΓΟΡΑ.

μὴ νυν πρότερον μηδεὶς ὑμῶν ἀντείπῃ μηδ᾽ ὑποκρούσῃ,
πρὶν ἐπίστασθαι τὴν ἐπίνοιαν καὶ τοῦ φράζοντος ἀκοῦσαι.
κοινωνεῖν γὰρ πάντας φήσω χρῆναι πάντων μετέχοντας,
κἀκ ταὐτοῦ ζῆν, καὶ μὴ τὸν μὲν πλουτεῖν, τὸν δ᾽ ἄθλιον εἶναι,
μηδὲ γεωργεῖν τὸν μὲν πολλὴν τῷ δ᾽ εἶναι μηδὲ ταφῆναι,
μηδ᾽ ἀνδραπόδοις τὸν μὲν χρῆσθαι πολλοῖς, τὸν δ᾽ οὐδ᾽
    ἀκολούθῳ·
ἀλλ᾽ ἕνα ποιῶ κοινὸν ἅπασιν βίοτον καὶ τοῦτον ὅμοιον.

ΒΛΕΠΥΡΟΣ.

πῶς οὖν ἔσται κοινὸς ἅπασιν ;

ΠΡΑΞΑΓΟΡΑ.

κατέδει πέλεθον πρότερός μου.

ΒΛΕΠΥΡΟΣ.

καὶ τῶν πελέθων κοινωνοῦμεν ;

ΠΡΑΞΑΓΟΡΑ.

μὰ Δί᾽, ἀλλ᾽ ἔφθης μ᾽ ὑποκρούσας.
τοῦτο γὰρ ἤμελλον ἐγὼ λέξειν· τὴν γῆν πρώτιστα ποιήσω
κοινὴν πάντων καὶ τἀργύριον καὶ τἄλλ᾽ ὁπόσ᾽ ἐστὶν ἑκάστῳ.
εἶτ᾽ ἀπὸ τούτων κοινῶν ὄντων ἡμεῖς βοσκήσομεν ὑμᾶς
ταμιευόμεναι, καὶ φειδόμεναι, καὶ τὴν γνώμην προσέχουσαι.

ΒΛΕΠΥΡΟΣ.

πῶς οὖν ὅστις μὴ κέκτηται γῆν ἡμῶν, ἀργύριον δὲ
καὶ Δαρεικούς, ἀφανῆ πλοῦτον ;

ARISTOPHANES. 53

ΠΡΑΞΑΓΟΡΑ.
τοῦτ' ἐς τὸ μέσον καταθήσει.

ΒΛΕΠΥΡΟΣ.
καὶ μὴ καταθεὶς ψευδορκήσει. κἀκτήσατο γὰρ διὰ τοῦτο.

ΠΡΑΞΑΓΟΡΑ.
ἀλλ' οὐδέν τοι χρήσιμον ἔσται πάντως αὐτῷ.

ΒΛΕΠΥΡΟΣ.
κατὰ δὴ τί;

ΠΡΑΞΑΓΟΡΑ.
οὐδεὶς οὐδὲν πενίᾳ δράσει· πάντα γὰρ ἕξουσιν ἅπαντες,
ἄρτους, τεμάχη, μάζας, χλαίνας, οἶνον, στεφάνους, ἐρεβίνθους.
606.
ARISTOPHANES, ΕΚΚΛΗΣΙΑΖΟΥΣΑΙ.

I will place some parts of these passages nearer together, so that the reader may more easily see the resemblance between the democracy of Praxagora and the commonwealths of Cade and Gonzalo, and the words of Aristophanes and Shakespeare.

All the realm shall be in common.

κοινωνεῖν γὰρ πάντας φήσω χρῆναι πάντων μετέχοντας.

τὴν γῆν πρώτιστα ποιήσω
κοινὴν πάντων καὶ τἀργύριον καὶ τἄλλ' ὁπόσ' ἐστὶν ἑκάστῳ.

There shall be in England seven halfpenny loaves sold for a penny.

πάντα γὰρ ἕξουσιν ἅπαντες,
ἄρτους.

No marrying among his subjects?
None, man; all idle: whores and knaves.

ΒΛΕΠΥΡΟΣ.

ἢν μείρακ' ἰδὼν ἐπιθυμήσῃ καὶ βούληται σκαλαθῦραι,
ἕξει τούτων ἀφελὼν ζοῦναι, τῶν ἐκ κοινοῦ δὲ μεθέξει
ξυγκαταδαρθών.

ΠΡΑΞΑΓΟΡΑ.

ἀλλ' ἐξέσται πρωΐκ' αὐτῷ ξυγκαταδαρθεῖν.
καὶ ταύτας γὰρ κοινὰς ποιῶ τοῖς ἀνδράσι συγκατακεῖσθαι
καὶ παιδοποιεῖν τῷ βουλομένῳ. 615.

ΕΚΚΛΗΣΙΑΖΟΥΣΑΙ.

Nature should bring forth,
Of its own kind, all foison, all *abundance*.

ΠΡΑΞΑΓΟΡΑ.

ἀλλ' οὐκ ἔσται τοῦτο παρ' ἡμῖν.
πᾶσι γὰρ ἄφθονα πάντα παρέξομεν. 690.

Mrs. Page. Here comes little Robin.

[*Enter* ROBIN.

Mrs. Ford. How now, my *eyas-musket?* what news
with you?

Merry Wives of Windsor, Act iii. Sc. 3.

Ham. How comes it? do they grow rusty?

Ros. Nay, their endeavour keeps in the wonted pace:
but there is, sir, an *aery* of children, little *eyases*, that *cry
out* on the top of question, and are most tyrannically
clapped for 't: these are now the fashion, and so berattle
the common stages—so they call them—that many
wearing rapiers are afraid of goose-quills, and dare
scarce come thither.

Hamlet, Act ii. Sc. 2.

Names are bestowed on a falcon according to her age or
taking. The first is an *eyess*, which name lasts as long as
she is in the *eyrie*. These are very troublesome in their

feeding, do *cry very much*, and are difficultly *entred*: but
being well entred and quarried, prove excellent hawks
for the hern, river, or any sort of fowl, and are hardy
and *full of mettle.—The Gentleman's Recreation.*

> *Horatio.* Now, sir, young Fortinbras,
> Of unimproved *mettle hot and full,*
> Hath in the skirts of Norway here and there
> Shark'd up a list of lawless resolutes,
> For food and diet, to some enterprise
> That hath a stomach in 't.
> *Hamlet,* Act i. Sc. 1.

A hawk is said to be *entered* when he begins
to kill; and Cominius, speaking of Coriolanus,
says:

> At sixteen years,
> When Tarquin made a head for Rome, he fought
> Beyond the mark of others : our then dictator,
> Whom with all praise I point at, saw him fight,
> When with his Amazonian chin he drove
> The bristled lips before him : he bestrid
> An o'er-pressed Roman, and i' the consul's view
> Slew three opposers : Tarquin's self he met,
> And struck him on his knee : in that day's feats,
> When he might act the woman in the scene,
> He proved best man i' the field, and for his meed
> Was brow-bound with the oak. His pupil age
> *Man-entered* thus, he waxed like a sea;
> And, in the brunt of seventeen battles since,
> He lurched all swords o' the garland.
> *Coriolanus,* Act ii. Sc. 2.

Having reclaimed her, thoroughly manned her, and
made her eager and sharp set, then you may venture
to feed her on her lure. But before you shew her the

lure you must consider these three things :—1. That she be bold in, and familiar with, company, and noways afraid of dogs and horses. 2. That she be *sharp set* and hungry, regarding the hour of the morning and evening when you will lure her. 3. And lastly, she must be clean within, and the lure must be well garnished with meat on both sides, and you must abscond yourself when you intend to give her the length of the lease.

Having seeled your hawk, fit her with a large easy hood, which you must take off and put on very often, watching her two nights, handling her frequently and gently about the head as aforesaid. When you perceive she hath no aversion to the hood, unseel her in an evening, by candle-light ; continue handling her softly, often hooding and unhooding her, until she takes no offence at the hood, and will patiently *endure handling.*

K. Hen. Then, good my lord, teach your cousin to consent to winking.

Bur. I will wink on her to consent, my lord, if you will teach her to know my meaning : for maids, well summered and warm kept, are like flies at Bartholomew-tide, blind, though they have their eyes ; and then they will *endure handling*, which before would not abide looking on.

Henry V. Act v. Sc. 2.

If your seeled hawk feeds well, abides the hood and handling without striking or biting, then by candle-light in an evening unseel her, and with your finger and spittle anoint the place where the seeling-thread was drawn through ; then hood her, and hold her on your fist all night, often hooding, unhooding, and handling her, stroking her gently about the things and body, giving her sometimes a bit or two, also liring and plumage.—*The Gentleman's Recreation.*

Lecturers get a great deal of money, because they preach the people tame; as a man *watches a hawk*, and then they do what they list with them.—SELDEN, *Table Talk : Lecturers.*

If you would *man* her well, you should *watch* her all the night, keeping her continually on your fist.

You must bear her continually upon your fist till she be thoroughly *manned*, causing her to feed in company.

Pandarus. Come, come, what need you blush? shame's a baby.—Here she is now : swear the oaths now to her, that you have sworn to me.—What, are you gone again? you must be watched ere you be made tame, must you?—*Troilus and Cressida*, Act iii. Sc. 2.

You must unhood her gently, giving her two or three bits, and putting on her hood again you must give her as much more ; and be sure that she is close seeled, and after three or four days lessen her diet : and when you go to bed set her on some pearch by you, that you may awaken her often in the night. This you must do till you observe her *grow tame* and gentle; and when you find she begins to feed eagerly, then give her a sheep's heart. And now you may begin to unhood her by day-time, but it must be far from company : first giving her a bit or two, then hood her again gently, and give her so much more. Be sure not to affright her with anything when you unhood her.

Pet. Thus have I politicly begun my reign,
And 'tis my hope to end successfully ;
My falcon now is *sharp*, and passing empty ;
And, till she stoop, she must not be full-gorged,
For then she never looks upon her lure.
Another way I have to *man my haggard*,
To make her come, and *know her keeper's call*,
That is,—to *watch her*, as we watch these kites,

That *bate* and beat, and will not be obedient.
She eat no meat to-day, nor none shall eat;
Last night she slept not, nor to-night she shall not.

> *Taming the Shrew*, Act iv. Sc. 1.

And when you perceive her to be acquainted with company, and that she is *sharp set*, unhood her and give her some meat, holding her just against your face and eyes, which will make her less afraid of the countenance of others.

Having manned your hawk so that she *feeds boldly, acquaint her with your voice*, whistle, and such words as falconers use.

When she feeds boldly, and knows your voice and whistle, then teach her to know her feeding, and to *bate* at it in this manner. Shew her some meat with your right hand, crying and luring to her aloud: if she bate or strike at it, then let her quickly and neatly *foot* it, and feed on it for four or five bits.

Sicilius.   The holy eagle
Stoop'd, as to *foot* us.

> *Cymbeline*, Act v. Sc. 4.

Being well reclaimed, let her sit upon a pearch; but every night keep her on the fist three or four hours, stroaking, hooding, and unhooding, &c., as aforesaid: and this you may do in the day-time, when she hath learned to feed eagerly without fear.—*The Gentleman's Recreation.*

Pandarus and Petrucio both refer to the watching and waking in training hawks. Petrucio alludes, also, to one of the things to be considered before you show the hawk her lure, namely, that she must be *sharp set* and hungry; and Shakespeare refers to the falconer's practice of manning hawks by hooding and unhooding them, when he makes *Juliet* say:

> Come, civil night,
> Thou sober-suited matron all in black,
> And learn me how to lose a winning match
> Play'd for a pair of stainless maidenhoods:
> Hood my *unmann'd* blood bating in my checks,
> With thy black mantle; till strange love, grown bold,
> Think true love acted simple modesty.
>
> Act iii. Sc. 2.

Moreover, in one of the extracts I have made from 'The Gentleman's Recreation,' it is said that, in manning a hawk, you must commence hooding and unhooding her by night, and that you may do this in the daytime, when she hath learned to feed without fear; and Juliet asks the night to hood her unmanned blood till strange love, grown bold, think true love acted simple modesty.

> *Constable.* By my faith, sir, but it is; never anybody saw it, but his lackey: 'tis a hooded valour; and, when it appears, it will bate.—*Henry V.*, Act iii. Sc. 7.

The word 'bate' used by Petrucio, Juliet, and Constable, is a term of art in falconry, thus explained in 'The Gentleman's Recreation'—
'Bate is when a hawk endeavoureth to fly from

the hand or pearch, being tied to either.' So
Juliet's unmanned blood flies to her cheeks, as
a hawk from the hand or pearch, that is, it is
unruly; and Juliet asks the night with her
black mantle to hood and thereby subdue her
unmanned blood; she may also wish her cheeks
to be concealed, for she elsewhere says:

> Thou know'st the mask of night is on my face,
> Else would a maiden blush bepaint my cheek.
> Act ii. Sc. 2.

If Falstaff, in the First Part of Henry IV.,
Act ii. Scene 3, uses the word ' bate ' as a falconer's term—

> Bardolph, am I not fallen away vilely since this last
> action? Do I not bate? Do I not dwindle? Why,
> my skin hangs about me like an old lady's loose
> gown. I am withered like an old apple John—

he must refer, not to the act of bating, but to
the effect which it produces upon the body;
for, according to ' The Gentleman's Recreation,'
hawks which are ' very great baters are very
small eaters; and a hawk or a man that eats
very little, will dwindle.'

King John.   Our discontented counties do revolt;
Our people quarrel with *obedience;*
Swearing *allegiance,* and the love of soul,
To stranger blood, to foreign royalty.

Act v. Sc. 1.

Queen Katherine.   Tongues spit their duties out, and
   cold hearts freeze
Allegiance in them ; their curses now
Live where their prayers did ; and it's come to pass,
That tractable *obedience* is a slave
To each incensèd will.

Henry VIII., Act i. Sc. 2.

The reader will perceive that Shakespeare uses the terms allegiance and obedience in connection with each other; and, according to Coke:

As the subject oweth to the king his true and faithful ligeance and obedience, so the sovereign is to govern and protect his subjects : regere et protegere subditos suos ; so as between the sovereign and subject there is duplex et reciprocum ligamen, quia sicut subditus regi tenetur ad obedientiam, ita rex subdito tenetur ad protectionem ; merito igitur ligeantia dicitur, a ligando, quid continet in se duplex ligamen.

And again :

This word ligeance is well expressed by divers several names or synonyma which we find in our books. Sometime it is called the obedience or obeysance of the subject to the king, obedientia regi.—*Co. Rep. Calvin's Case.*

Oswald. Help, ho ! murder ! help !
Kent. Strike, you slave; stand, rogue, stand ; you neat slave, strike.

                                    Lear, Act ii. Sc. 2.

Kent calls the steward a neat slave, and there was neat land, *terra villanorum,* which was land let or granted out to yeomanry; therefore it may be considered probable that the word used by Kent is not the adjective 'neat,' Italian *netto,* French *net,* Latin *nitidus, niteo,* to shine, to be clean, fair, or fine, but that Kent uses the substantive 'neat,' derived from the Saxon *neat, neten, niten, nyten,* which signifies black cattle—beeves, as oxen, heifers, *calves* and steers.

Leontes. Why, that's my bawcock. What, hast smutch'd
        thy nose ?—
They say, it's a copy out of mine. Come, captain,
We must be neat ; not neat, but cleanly, captain :
And yet the steer, the heifer, and the calf,
Are all call'd neat.

                                Winter's Tale, Act i. Sc. 2.

The word 'neat' seems to be used by Leontes in a double sense : we must be 'neat,' that is, clean, trim; and yet we must not be 'neat,' that is, unclean, like 'the steer, the heifer, and the calf,' or those who tend them. It is evident that Leontes uses the adjective 'neat,' signifying clean, trim, &c., and also the substantive 'neat,' derived from the Saxon, in the sense of unclean, or at least in a sense which implies the condition of which the adjective 'unclean' is descriptive—a condition common to 'the steer, the heifer, and the calf,' and those who tended them, as tenants of neat land. Because Leontes uses the word 'neat' in a sense implying the uncleanliness which is common to cattle, or those who tend them, therefore I have thought it probable that Kent may mean, by using the words 'neat slave,' that Oswald, the steward, was like a tenant of neat land, that is, a base, dirty fellow. It may be considered doubtful whether the word 'neat' used by Kent is the substantive 'neat,' signifying one who was a tenant of neat land; but if Kent does use that substantive, he probably uses it in an adjective sense, in connection with the word 'slave,' in the same manner as Shakespeare, in 'Henry VI.' Part 2, seems to use the substantive 'dunghill' in an adjective sense, in connection with the word 'villain.'

York. Base dunghill villain, and mechanical,
I'll have thy head for this thy traitor's speech.
Act i. Sc. 3.

Bigot. Out, dunghill! darest thou brave a nobleman?
King John, Act iv. Sc. 3.

Oswald. Out, dunghill!
Lear, Act iv. Sc. 6.

Littleton thus describes the villein service to which Shakespeare may allude in these passages:

Tenure in villenage is most properly when a villein holdeth of his lord, to whom he is a villein, certain lands or tenements according to the custom of the mannor, or otherwise, at the will of the lord, and to do his lord villein service; as to carry and re-carry *dung* of his lord out of the city, or out of his lord's mannor, unto the land of his lord, and to spread the same upon the land, and such like.—Section 172.

Rosaline. A jest's prosperity lies in the ear
Of him that hears it, never in the tongue
Of him that makes it.
Love's Labour's Lost, Act v. Sc. 2.

καίτοι ἔγωγ᾽ ὁρῶ τῆς τῶν λεγόντων δυνάμεως τοὺς ἀκούοντας τὸ πλεῖστον κυρίους· ὡς γὰρ ἂν ὑμεῖς ἀποδέξησθε καὶ πρὸς ἕκαστον ἔχητ᾽ εὐνοίας, οὕτως ὁ λέγων ἔδοξε φρονεῖν.
—DEMOSTHENES, ΠΕΡΙ ΤΟΥ ΣΤΕΦΑΝΟΥ.

The Thanes who possessed bocland divided them according to the proportion of their estates into two sorts, inland and outland,

inlantal, inlantale, demesne or inland, to
which was opposed delantal'-land, tenanted
or outland. 'Abbat et Conventus Glaston.
concesserunt vicario de Suppiwike decimas
bladi omnium croftarum tunc existentium,
duntaxat quæ non sunt Inlandtal in tota pa-
rochia de Suppiwike, eo quod omnes hæ
croftæ sunt Delantal.' (Chartular. Abbat.
Glaston. M.S. f. 115 b.) 'Inland, Inlandum,
terra Dominicalis, pars manerii Dominica,
terra interior;' for that which was let out to
the tenants was called utland. In the Tes-
tament of Brithericus, in Itiner. Cantii, 'tis
said thus according to Lambert's interpretation—'To Hulfee (I give) the inland or de-
means, and to Elfeyth outland or tenancy.'
This word is often found in Doomsday.
(Cowell.) The inland was that which lay
next, or most convenient for, the lord's mansion-house, as within the view thereof, and
therefore they kept that part in their own
hands for the support of themselves and their
families. The Normans afterwards called
these lands terræ dominicales, the demains, or
lord's lands.

Orl.   Are you native of this place ?

Ros.   As the coney, that you see dwell where she is kindled.

Orl.   Your accent is something finer than you could purchase in so removed a dwelling.

Ros.   I have been told so of many: but, indeed, an old religious uncle of mine taught me to speak, who was in his youth an *inland* man: one that knew courtship too well, for there he fell in love.

As You Like It, Act iii. Sc. 2.

It appears to me reasonable to conclude that there would be more refinement of manners and of speech, or, as Orlando says, of 'accent,' in one who was 'inland' bred, that is, brought up on the demesnes or demain lands of the lord, and subject necessarily to the influence of whatever degree of refinement there may have been in the society formed by the lord's family, his guests and retainers, than in one who was 'outland' bred, that is, brought up on land which was not next to the lord's mansion-house, but remote therefrom.   I am inclined to think that the word 'removed,' used by Orlando, refers to the 'outland,' because Rosalind immediately afterwards makes use of the word 'inland,' to which it is opposed in meaning, and she says, in effect, 'The reason my accent is something finer than could be acquired in so removed a dwelling, as I have been told of many, is this—that an old uncle of mine taught me to speak, who was in his youth an inland man.' If, for the reasons I have stated, it should be considered probable that the tenants of the inland were more refined than the tenants of the outland, it may then also be considered probable that, in course of time, all persons who resembled the tenants of the outland in their want of refinement, were designated by the term 'outlandish,' an adjective which is often applied in England at the present day to those who are rude in manner and in speech.

Polonius. He closes with you in this consequence:
'Good sir,' or so, or 'friend,' or 'gentleman,'
According to the phrase or the addition
Of man and country.

Hamlet, Act ii. Sc. 1.

The description of an individual in a legal document as esquire, gentleman, yeoman, &c., is called his addition, and Shakespeare frequently uses this word 'addition' in its legal sense.

King. Where great additions swell, and virtue none,
It is a dropsied honour: good alone
Is good, without a name.

All's Well that Ends Well, Act ii. Sc. 3.

So Angelo says:

> Thieves for their robbery have authority,
> When judges steal themselves.
>   *Measure for Measure*, Act ii. Sc. 2.

It may be said of the addition ' esquire,' that in England there is no title more unwarrantably assumed or more indiscriminately applied,

> So common-hackney'd in the eyes of men,
> So stale and cheap to vulgar company.

Esquire (French *écuyer* ; Italian *scudiere*, from the Latin *scutum*, a shield; from the Greek σκῦτος, a hide, of which shields were anciently made, and afterwards covered, for in the time of the Anglo-Saxons the shields were covered with leather) signified originally he who attended a knight in time of war and carried his shield, whence he was called escuier in French, and scutifer or armiger, that is, armour-bearer, in Latin.   So Shakespeare makes Falstaff say, playing on the word ' night':

> Marry, then, sweet wag, when thou art king, let not us, that are *squires of the night's body*, be called thieves of the day's beauty ; let us be—Diana's foresters, gentlemen of the shade, minions of the moon.—1 *Henry IV.*, Act i. Sc. 2.

> *Shal.*   Sir Hugh, persuade me not ; I will make a Star-chamber matter of it : if he were twenty Sir John Falstaffs, he shall not abuse Robert Shallow, esquire.

Slen. In the county of Gloucester, justice of peace and ' Coram.'

Shal. Ay, cousin Slender, and 'Custalorum.'

Slen. Ay, and ' Rato-lorum' too ; and a gentleman born, master parson ; who writes himself ' Armigero,' in any bill, warrant, quittance, or obligation, 'Armigero.'

Merry Wives of Windsor, Act i. Sc. 1.

Slender speaks of Shallow's right to describe himself armigero in any bill, &c.; and Macbeth, in answer to the assurance of the first murderer, ' we are men, my liege,' says:

Macb. Ay, in the catalogue ye go for men ;
As hounds, and greyhounds, mongrels, spaniels, curs,
Shoughs, water-rugs, and demi-wolves, are cleped
All by the name of dogs : the valued file
Distinguishes the swift, the slow, the subtle,
The house-keeper, the hunter, every one
According to the gift which bounteous nature
Hath in him closed ; whereby he does receive
Particular addition, from the bill
That writes them all alike: and so of men.

Act iii. Sc. 1.

The bill to which Macbeth and Shallow refer may be an indictment, which is a bill or declaration of complaint, that is, drawn up and exhibited for some criminal or penal offence, and preferred to the grand jury or inquest of the county, upon whose oaths (taken before proper judges having power to punish or certify the offence) they are to find whether the complaint in the indictment is true or not. Therein must be set forth (*inter alia*) the Christian name, surname, and *addition* of the offender, &c.

Armiger, in English, signifies esquire, and perhaps an esquire may be called armiger quasi armigerens, from his bearing arms. Ancient writers and chronologers make mention of some who are called armigeri, whose office was to carry the shield of some nobleman. Camden calls them scutiferi, which seems to import as much, and homines ad arma delecti. (Noy's Max.)

Custos Rotulorum is an officer who has the custody of the rolls and records of the sessions of the peace, and also, as some authorities state, of the commission of the peace itself. He is constantly a justice of the peace and quorum in the county where his office is kept.

Quorum (Latin, ' of whom ') is a word frequently used in the commissions of the justices of the peace, as where a commission is directed to five or seven persons, or to any three of them, among whom B. C. and D. E. are said to be of the quorum, because the rest cannot proceed without them. And thence a justice

of the peace and quorum is one without whom
the rest of the judges cannot act in some
cases.

———————

Second Clown. The *crowner* hath sat on her and finds
it Christian burial.

* * * * * *

Second Clown. But is this law ?
First Clown. Ay, marry is 't; *crowner's-quest* law.

Hamlet, Act v. Sc. 1.

Beside these officers afore mentioned, there are sun-
dric other in everic countie, as *crowners*, whose dutie is
to inquire of such as cerne to their death by violence,
to attach and present the plees of the crowne, to make
inquirie of treasure found, &c. There are divers also of
the best learned of the law, beside sundrie gentlemen,
where the number of lawiers will not suffice (and whose
revenues doo amount to above twentie pounds by the
yeare), appointed by especiall commission from the prince,
to looke unto the good government of his subjects, in
the counties where they dwell.

Slender. In the county of Gloucester, justice of peace,
and 'Coram.'

Merry Wives, Act i. Sc. 1.

And of these the least skilfull in the law are of tho
peace, the other both of the peace and quorum, otherwise
called of Oier and Determiner; so that the first have
authoritie onelie to hear, the other to heare and deter-
mine such matters as are brought unto their presence.
These also direct their warrants to the keepers of the gailes
within their limitations, for the safe keeping of such
offenders as they shall judge worthie to commit unto
their custodie, there to be kept under ward, until the great
assises, to the end their causes may be further examined

before the residue of the countie; and these officers were first devised about the eighteene yeare of Edward the Third, as I have beene informed.—HOLINSHED, *The Description of England*, Chap. 1.

The word 'crowner,' used in 'Hamlet,' is, I think, generally supposed to be a corruption of the Clown's, but it is merely the English of the Law Latin *coronator*, from *corona*, a crown, which Holinshed also uses. Slender says, in effect, that Justice Shallow was the most skilful in the law, because he was not merely justice of peace, but also of the quorum; and Holinshed says, 'the least skilfull in the law are of the peace, the other both of the peace and quorum.'

Selden says:

The title of esquire or armiger is between the dignity of knight-bachelor and the common title of gentleman. And it is of that nature with us now, that to whomsoever, either by blood, place in the state, or other eminence, we conceive some higher attribute should be given than the sole title gentleman, knowing yet that he hath no other honorary title legally fixed on him, we usually style him an esquire, in such passages as require legally that his degree or estate be mentioned, as especially in indictments and actions whereupon he may be outlawed.—*Tit. Hon.*

As a name of estate or degree it was used in divers Acts of Parliament before and after the 1 Henry V. cap. 5 for Rot. Parl. and 1 E. 4.

John Audeley, an ancient and noble baron, was named Johannes Audeley, Armiger, for that all the rest of the barons that appeared at that Parliament were knights. (2 Inst. 667.) Under Richard II. we find the name of esquire expressly given as a created and honorary title by patent. One John de Kingston was so by this patent received into the state of a gentleman, and made an esquire by King Richard II.; and it might be reasonably conceived that the title of esquire was then only such as was either thus created, or otherwise acquired by service or employment. (Selden, Tit. Hon.) In 1413, Dr. Fuller says that John Golope was the first person who assumed the title of an esquire, and that until the end of Henry VI.'s reign such distinctions were not used except in law proceedings; but Ordericus Vitalis, as early as 1124, speaks of the Earl of Mellent, who, endeavouring to escape from the troops of Henry Beauclerc, and being seized by a countryman, bribed him to set him free. and to shave him in the guise of an esquire, 'instar armigeri.'

by which means he eluded his pursuers.
From the time of Henry V., when the Statute
of Additions was passed, it often occurs as a
legal addition ; and long before the reign of
Henry VI. it was a general name with us,
for such as were, it seems, by their military
employment, *militaris ordinis candidati*, and
being beneath knights-bachelors, were either
attendant on them or some greater persons, or
employed otherwise in the wars under that
name, or had it by creation. Hence it is that
in Froissart we have so frequently chivalers
and esquires to express the best part of the
army, and the like of milites and armigeri.
Chaucer mentions the attendance of the esquire on the knight in his description in the
Prologue to the ' Canterbury Tales ' :

> Curteys he was, lowly, and servysable,
> And carf byforn his fadur at the table.

And also in the ' Merchant's Tale ' :

> The tyme cam that resoun was to ryse,
> And after that men daunce, and drynke fast,
> And spices al about the hous thay cast,
> And ful of joy and bliss is every man,
> Al but a squier, that hight Damyan,
> Which karf before the knight ful many a day.

And, says Selden, for the necessary attendance of an esquire upon every knight in the
elder ages, long before Chaucer, observe this
of Sir Francis Tias: his recovering five pound
damages, under Edward I., in Wakefield Court,
in Yorkshire, against one German Mercer,
for arresting the horse of one William Lepton,
that was his esquire, and so making him to
be unattended. 'France Tyas, miles' (so are
the words of the court-roll) 'tulit actionem
versus Germanum Mercer, qui arrestavit
equum Willielmi Lepton armigeri sui ad dede-
cus et damnum prædicti Franci, quia fuit sine
armigero. Et prædictus Franco recuperavit c.
solidos. Ideo Germanus Mercer sit in miseri-
cordia.' Under the reign of Henry IV., in our
year-books the plaintiff had been bound by
indentures to be the defendant's esquire in
time of peace, and it seems plain, says Selden,
that by this time (MCCCCI.) the title was
fixed on some, without any reference to the
words, but only by service on great persons.
For of the witnesses examined in that great case
between the Lord Gray of Ruthen and the
Lord Hastings, under the same king, one John
Lee of Buckingham is titled esquire, as many

more are; and it is said of him, as from his
own mouth, that he was a gentleman by birth,
and had land of twenty marks by descent, 'et
n'ad use point de travailer en guerre ne son
pier devant luy, et pour ce ne prist gard d'ap-
prendre ses armes;' for he should have an-
swered to the questions whether he were a
gentleman and had arms or no. And in truth
this John Lee was retained to that Lord Ruthen
as surveyor of his lands for a time, and besides of perpetual fee with him for other ser-
vices, whence it seems he was called esquire;
and for some like cause perhaps all the rest,
or the most that in those examinations have
that title, for many there have it, were styled
so. The Lord Rivers also, under Henry V.,
devises by his will that his feofees should make
an estate ' Thomæ Gower, armigero meo.'

I do not recollect an authority for the pre-
valent opinion that every gentleman possessing
landed property worth three hundred pounds
a year, or any other sum, is therefore entitled
to this degree, unless this passage in Selden,
about John Lee of Buckingham, be considered
as such; and, from all the authorities with
which I am familiar, it seems evident that no

real or personal estate whatsoever will entitle
its possessor to the addition esquire. Although
King John says,

Go, Faulconbridge ; now hast thou thy desire,
A landless knight makes thee a landed squire,
Act i. Sc. 1.

it is not certain that Shakespeare means Faulconbridge was a squire because he had land.

In the ancient creation of the dignity, says
Selden, when such as otherwise had it not were
created into it, it is noted that a collar of SS.
was given by the king as an ensign of it received. Justice Newton, under Henry VI.,
said : 'If a writ of debt be brought against the
Sergeant of the Kitchen in the king's house.
I may call him cook, and my writ is good
enough, and yet he hath a collar and is a
gentleman.' He uses the word 'gentleman.'
applying it to those that were so made esquires
by the king's favour, because also they were
by their creation put in the rank of the most
eminent sort of gentlemen on whom the title of
esquire hath since been so fixed. (Tit. Hon.)
The persons entitled to this degree by the English law are, according to various authorities, the
sons of all the peers and lords of Parliament,

(2 Inst. 667; 2 Vin. Abr. 84, pl. 28); the
eldest sons of peers, and their eldest sons in
perpetual succession (Selden, Tit. Hon. Dod.
Nob. 144), and, consequently, the younger
sons of peers after the death of their fathers
(Cowel, Interp. Tit. Esquire), both which speices
of esquiers Sir Henry Spelman entitles armigeri
natalitii (Gloss. 3); all dukes, marquesses,
earles, viscounts, and barons of other nations,
or which are not lords of the Parliament of
England, are named armigeri, if they be no
knights; and if knights, then are they named
milites (2 Inst. 667); the eldest sons of
baronets (Cowel, Interp.); the eldest sons of
knights (2 Inst. 667), and their eldest sons for
ever (Selden, Tit. Hon. Dod. Nob.); esquires
created expressly with a collar of SS. and
spurs of silver (Spelman, Gloss. verbo Armigeri),
of whom there are none at present; persons to
whom the king gives arms by letters patent,
with the title esquire, and their eldest sons for
ever (Selden, Tit. Hon. Com. Dig. b. viii.);
esquires of knights of the Bath, each of whom
formerly constituted two at installation, and at
present three (Statutes of the Order of the
Bath, p. 32); barristers-at-law (Cowel, Spelman, and 1 Wils, 245).

Sir Henry Spelman says, 'Certe altero hinc sæculo nominatissimus in patriâ jurisconsul-tus, ætate provectior, etiam munere gaudens publico et prædiis amplissimis generosi titulo, bene se habuit; forte, quod togatæ genti magis tunc conveniret civilis illa appellatio quam castrensis altera.' (Gloss. voce Arm.) But whether barristers-at-law, as such, are esquires or not, their long assumption of the title seems to have established such a right to the distinction that, many years ago, the Court of Common Pleas refused to hear an affidavit read because the barrister therein named had not the addition esquire to his name (1 Wils. 244); and it is said that, about the same time, Mr. Justice Heath refused knighthood, saying, 'I am John Heath, Esquire, one of his Majesty's Justices of the Court of Common Bench, and so will die.' And Shallow, in answer to Bar-dolph's enquiry, 'Which is Justice Shallow?' says:

Shal. I am Robert Shallow, sir; a poor esquire of this county, and one of the king's justices of the peace.
2 *Henry IV.*, Act iii. Sc. 2.

According to Blount, those to whom this title is now of right due, are all the younger sons of noblemen, and their heirs male for

ever ; the four esquires of the king's body;
the eldest sons of baronets ; so also of all
knights of the Bath and knights-bachelors,
and their heirs male in right line; those that
serve the king in any worshipful calling, as
the sergeant chirurgeon, sergeant of the ewry,
master cook, &c.; and such as are created
esquires by the king with a collar of SS. of
silver, as the heralds and sergeants-at-arms.
The chiefs of some ancient families are like-
wise esquires by prescription; those that bear
any superior office in the commonwealth, as
high sheriff of any county, who retains the
title of esquire during his life, in respect of
the great trust he has had of the posse comi-
tatus.   He who is a justice of the peace has it
during the time he is in commission, and no
longer, if not otherwise qualified to bear it.
Utter barristers, in Acts of Parliament for
poll money, were ranked among esquires.   In
all the British colonies, except Jamaica and
Barbadoes, attorneys, as they unite in their
practice the distinct departments of attorney
and counsel, are styled esquires. (1 Bla. Com.
342, note to Williams' edition.)   Justices of
the peace while in commission, but not justices

of the peace of corporate towns (Cowel and
1 Wils. 244, sed quære), persons chosen
esquires to the body of the Prince (Selden,
Tit. Hon.), of whom at present there are none ;
persons attending on the King's or Queen's
corporation in some employment, or persons
employed in any superior office under the
Crown, and who are styled esquires by the
King in their commissions and appointments
(Selden, Tit. Hon. Dod. Nob. 144) ; such, for
instance, as sheriffs of counties and captains
and superior officers in the army and navy
(1 Bla. Com. 406, note to Christian's edition) ;
but officers in the militia and volunteers are
not, it seems, entitled to this addition. Talbot
and Eagle, April 21, 1809, was an action
brought against the defendant to recover the
penalty of £5 given by the statute of 5 Anne,
c. xiv. s. 4, for killing game, not being duly
qualified. Upon the trial of this cause, before
Grose J. at Suffolk spring assizes, the defendant, to prove his qualification, gave in
evidence a commission signed by the lord-
lieutenant of the county of Suffolk, con-
stituting the defendant's father the captain
commandant of a corps of volunteer infantry,

and styling him an esquire, and also the
Gazette announcing his appointment, and he
relied on the statute 54 Geo. III. c. liv. s. 26,
which enacts that all officers in corps of volunteers, having commissions from lieutenants of
counties, shall rank with the officers of his
Majesty's forces. The jury found a verdict
for the plaintiff. Shepherd (Sergeant) now
moved to set aside the verdict, and enter a
nonsuit, contending that the defendant's father
had by this appointment been created an
esquire. But the court was clearly of opinion
that the statute meant only the same military
rank ; the lord-lieutenant of the county could
not confer honours ; there was no pretence to
call this gentleman an esquire, and they refused the rule. (1 Taunt. Rep.) From this
decision it seems that lieutenants in the
navy and the Guards, who rank as captains, are not, therefore, entitled to this
degree. I have quoted most of the authorities with which I am familiar, and they are
sometimes conflicting; for example, Camden,
in his description of an esquire, after men-
tioning the persons entitled to the degree,
states that others who bear any office of trust

under the Crown are also entitled thereto. But Christian, in a note on Blackstone, observes that this description is too extensive, for it would bestow it on every exciseman and custom-house officer; and the learned Selden, perhaps the greatest authority on this subject, does not support the assertion of Camden. It seems that the addition esquire should be limited to those entitled thereto by birth or creation, or to those who are styled esquires by the Queen in their commissions and appointments; yet, according to Selden and Blount, it is sometimes found in the kitchen! But whoever may or may not be entitled to the addition of esquire, of this there can be no doubt, that

> A king can make a belted knight,
> A marquis, duke, and a' that;
> But an honest man's aboon his might,
> Guid faith he maunna fa' that!
> For a' that and a' that,
> Their dignities, and a' that;
> The pith o' sense and pride o' worth
> Are higher ranks than a' that.

An enquiry of this kind may be concluded with a few words from the Epilogus to Littleton's 'Tenures':

Know that I would not have thee believe that all which I have said in these books is law, for I will not presume to take this upon me. But of those things that are not law, enquire and learn of my wise masters learned in the law.

END OF THE FIRST PART.

LONDON

PRINTED BY SPOTTISWOODE AND CO.

NEW-STREET SQUARE.

www.ingramcontent.com/pod-product-compliance
Lightning Source LLC
Chambersburg PA
CBHW031445270326
41930CB00007B/874